# Werwolves

Werwolves
Author: Elliot O'Donnell

Cover image: *Jupiter and Lycaon,* Jan Cossiers (1636 - 1638)
Lay-out: www.burokd.nl

ISBN 978-94-92355-50-8

VAMzzz Publishing
P.O. Box 3340
1001 AC Amsterdam
The Netherlands
www.vamzzz.com
vamzzz@protonmail.com

# WERWOLVES

Elliot O'Donnell

Elliott O'Donnell
Clifton, 27 February 1872 – Clevedon, North Somerset, 8 May 1965

## contents

CHAPTER I

# What is a Werwolf?

WHAT IS A WERWOLF? To this there is no one very satisfactory reply. There are, indeed, so many diverse views held with regard to the nature and classification of werwolves, their existence is so keenly disputed, and the subject is capable of being regarded from so many standpoints, that any attempt at definition in a restricted sense would be well-nigh impossible.

The word werwolf (or werewolf) is derived from the Anglo-Saxon *wer*, man, and *wulf*, wolf, and has its equivalents in the German *Währwolf* and French *loup-garou*, whilst it is also to be found in the languages, respectively, of Scandinavia, Russia, Austria-Hungary, the Balkan Peninsula, and of certain of the countries of Asia and Africa; from which it may be concluded that its range is pretty well universal.

Indeed, there is scarcely a country in the world in which belief in a werwolf, or in some other form of lycanthropy, has not once existed, though it may have ceased to exist now. But whereas in some countries the werwolf is considered wholly physical, in others it is looked upon as partly, if not entirely, superphysical. And whilst in some countries it is restricted to the male sex, in others it is confined to the female; and, again, in others it is to be met with in both sexes.

Hence, when asked to describe a werwolf, or what is generally believed to be a werwolf, one can only say that a werwolf is an anomaly—sometimes man, sometimes woman (or in the guise of man or woman); sometimes adult, sometimes child (or in the guise of such)—that, under certain conditions, possesses the property of metamorphosing into a wolf, the change being either temporary or permanent.

This, perhaps, expresses most of what is general concerning werwolves. For more particular features, upon which I will touch later, one must look to locality and time.

Those who are sceptical with regard to the existence of the werwolf, and refuse to accept, as proof of such existence, the accumulated testimony of centuries, attribute the origin of the belief in the phenomenon merely to an insane delusion, which, by reason of its novelty, gained a footing and attracted followers.

Humanity, they say, has ever been the same; and any fresh idea—no matter how bizarre or monstrous, so long as it is monstrous enough—has always met with support and won credence.

In favour of this argument it is pointed out that in many of the cases of persons accused of werwolfery, tried in France, and elsewhere, in the middle of the sixteenth century, when belief in this species of lycanthropy was at its zenith, there was an extraordinary readiness among the accused to confess, and even to give circumstantial evidence of their own metamorphosis; and that this particular form of self-accusation at length became so popular among the leading people in the land, that the judicial court, having its suspicions awakened, and, doubtless, fearful of sentencing so many important personages, acquitted the majority of the accused, announcing them to be the victims of delusion and hysteria.

Now, if it were admitted, argue these sceptics, that the bulk of so-called werwolves were impostors, is it not reasonable to suppose that all so-called werwolves were either voluntary or involuntary impostors?—the latter, *i.e.*, those who were not self-accused, being falsely accused by persons whose motive for so doing was revenge. For parallel cases one has only to refer to the trials for sorcery and witchcraft in England. And with regard to false accusations of lycanthropy—accusations founded entirely on hatred of the accused person—how easy it was to trump up testimony and get the accused convicted. The witnesses were rarely, if ever, subjected to a searching examination; the court was always biased, and a confession of guilt, when not voluntary—as in the case of the prominent citizen, when it was invariably pronounced due to hysteria or delusion—could always be obtained by means of torture, though a confession thus obtained, needless to say, is completely nullified. Moreover, we have no record of metamorphosis taking place in court, or before witnesses chosen for their impartiality. On the contrary, the alleged transmutations always occurred in obscure places, and in the presence of people who, one has reason to believe, were both hysterical and imaginative, and therefore predisposed to see wonders. So says this order of sceptic, and, to my mind, he says a great deal more than his facts justify; for although contemporary writers generally are agreed that a large percentage of those people who voluntarily confessed they were werwolves were mere dissemblers, there is no recorded conclusive testimony to show that all such self-accused persons were shams and delusionaries. Besides, even if such testimony were forthcoming, it would in nowise preclude the existence of the werwolf.

Nor does the fact that all the accused persons submitted to the rack, or other modes of torture, confessed themselves werwolves prove that all such confessions were false.

Granted also that some of the charges of lycanthropy were groundless, being based on malice—which, by the by, is no argument for the non-existence of lycanthropy, since it is acknowledged that accusations of all sorts, having been based on malice, have been equally groundless—there is nothing in the nature of written evidence that would justify one in assuming that all such charges were traceable to the same cause, *i.e.*, a malicious agency. Neither can one dismiss the testimony of those who swore they were actual eye-witnesses of metamorphoses, on the mere assumption that all such witnesses were liable to hallucination or hysteria, or were hyper-imaginative.

Testimony to an event having taken place must be regarded as positive evidence of such an occurrence, until it can be satisfactorily proved to be otherwise—and this is where the case of the sceptic breaks down; he can only offer assumption, not proof.

Another view, advanced by those who discredit werwolves, is that belief in the existence of such an anomaly originates in the impression made on man in early times by the great elemental powers of nature. It was, they say, man's contemplation of the changes of these great elemental powers of nature, *i.e.*, the changes of the sun and moon, wind, thunder and lightning, of the day and night, sunshine and rain, of the seasons, and of life and death, and his deductions therefrom, that led to his belief in and worship of gods that could assume varying shapes, such, for example, as India (who occasionally took the form of a bull), Derketo (who sometimes metamorphosed into a fish), Poseidon, Jupiter Ammon, Milosh Kobilitch, Minerva, and countless others—and that it is to this particular belief and worship, which is to be found in the mythology of every race, that all religions, as well as belief in fairies, demons, werwolves, and phantasms, may be traced.

Well, this might be so, if there were not, in my opinion, sufficient accumulative corroborative evidence to show that not only were there such anomalies as werwolves formerly, but that, in certain restricted areas, they are even yet to be encountered.

Taking, then, the actual existence of werwolves to be an established fact, it is, of course, just as impossible to state their origin as it is to state the origin of any other extraordinary form of creation. Every religious creed, every Occult sect, advances its own respective views—and has a perfect right to do so, as long as it advances them as views and not dogmatisms.

I, for my part, bearing in mind that everything appertaining to the creation of man and the universe is a profound mystery, cannot see the object on the part of religionists and scientists in being arbitrary with regard to a subject which any child of ten will apprehend to be one whereon it is futile to do other than theorize. My own theory, or rather one of my own theories, is that the property of transmutation, *i.e.*, the power of assuming any animal guise, was one of the many properties—including second sight, the property of becoming invisible at will, of divining the presence of water, metals, the advent of death, and of projecting the etherical body—which were bestowed on man at the time of his creation; and that although mankind in general is no longer possessed of them, a few of these properties are still, in a lesser degree, to be found among those of us who are termed psychic.

The history of the Jews is full of references to certain of these properties. The greatest of all the Superphysical Forces—the creating Force (the Hebrew Jah, Jehovah)—so says the Bible, constantly held direct communication with His elect—with Adam, Noah, Abraham, and Moses, while His emissaries, the angels, or what modern Occultists would term Benevolent Elementals, conversed with Abraham, Sarah, Jacob, and hosts of others. In this same history, too, there is no lack of reference to sorcery; and whilst Black Magic is illustrated in the tricks wrought by the magicians before Pharaoh, and the infliction of all manner of plagues upon the Egyptians, one is rather inclined to attribute to White Magic Daniel's safety among the lions; Shadrach, Meshach, and Abed-nego's preservation from the flames; Elijah's miraculous spinning out of the barrel of meal and cruse of oil, in the days of famine, and his raising of the widow's son. Also, to the account of White Magic—and should anyone dispute this point let me remind him that it is merely a difference in the point of view—I would add Elisha's calling up of the bears that made such short work of the naughty children who tormented him. There are, too, many examples of divination recorded in the Bible. In Genesis, chapter xxx., verses 27-43, a description is given of a divining rod and its influence over sheep and other animals; in Exodus, chapter xvii., verse 15, Moses with the aid of a rod discovers water in the rock at Rephidim, and for similar instances one has only to refer to Exodus, chapter xiv., verse 16, and chapter xvii., verses 9-11. The calling up of the phantasm of Samuel at Endor more than suggests a biblical precedent for the modern practice of spiritualism; and it was, undoubtedly, the abuse of such power as that possessed by the witch of Endor, and the prevalence of sorcery, such as she practised, that finally led to the decree delivered by Moses to the Children of Israel, that on no account were they to suffer a witch to live. Reference to yet another property of the occult—namely, Etherical Projection—which is clearly exemplified in the Scriptures, may be found in Numbers, chapter xii., verse 6; in Job, chapter xxxiii., verse 15; in the First Book of Kings, chapter iii., verse 5; in Genesis, chapter xx., verses 3 and 6, and chapter xxxi., verse 24; in Isaiah, Jeremiah, Nahum, and Zechariah; and more particularly in the Acts of the Apostles, and in the Revelation of St. John. Lastly, in this history of the Jews, which is surely neither more nor less authenticated than any other well established history, testimony as to the existence of one species of Elemental of much the same order as the werwolf is recorded by Isaiah. In chapter xiii., verse 21, we read: "And their houses shall be full of doleful creatures, and owls shall dwell there, and satyrs shall dance there." Satyrs! we repeat; are not satyrs every whit as grotesque and outrageous as werwolves? Why, then, should those who, regarding the Scriptures as infallible, confess to a belief in the satyr, reject the possibility of a werwolf? And for those who are more logically sceptical—who question the veracity of the Bible and are dubious as to its authenticity—there are the chronicles of Herodotus, Petronius Arbiter, Baronius, Dôle, Olaus Magnus, Marie de France, Thomas Aquinas, Richard Verstegan, and many other recognized historians and classics, covering a large area in the history of man, all of whom specially testify to the existence—in their own respective periods—of werwolves.

And if any further evidence of this once near relationship with the Other World is required, one has only to turn to Aristotle, who wrote so voluminously on psychic dreams (most of which I am inclined to think were due to projection); to the teachings of Pythagoras and his followers, Empedocles and Apollonius; to Cicero and Tacitus; to Virgil, who frequently talks of ghosts and seers of Tyana; to Plato, the exponent of magic; and to Plutarch, whose works swarm with allusions to Occultism of all kinds—phantasms of the dead, satyrs, and numerous other species of Elementals.

I say, then, that in ages past, before any of the artificialities appertaining to our present mode of living were introduced; when the world was but thinly populated and there were vast regions of wild wastes and silent forests, the Known and Unknown walked hand in hand. It was seclusion of this kind, the seclusion of nature, that spirits loved, and it was in this seclusion they were always to be found whenever man wanted to hold communication with them. To such silent spots—to the woods and wildernesses—Buddha, Mohammed, the Hebrew Patriarchs and Prophets, all, in their turn, resorted, to solicit the companionship of benevolently disposed spirits, to be tutored by them, and, in all probability, to receive from them additional powers. To these wastes and forests, too, went all those who wished to do ill. There they communed with the spirits of darkness, *i.e.*, demons, or what are also termed Vice Elementals; and from the latter they acquired—possibly in exchange for some of their own vitality, for spirits of this order are said to have envied man his material body—tuition in sorcery, and such properties as second sight, invisibility, and lycanthropy.

This property of lycanthropy, or metamorphosing into a beast, probably dates back to man's creation. It was, I am inclined to believe, conferred on man at his creation by Malevolent Forces that were antagonistic to man's progress; and that these Malevolent Forces had a large share in the creation of this universe is, to my mind, extremely probable. But, however that may be, I cannot believe that the creation of man and the universe were due entirely to one Creator—there are assuredly too many inconsistencies in all we see around us to justify belief in only one Creative Force. The Creator who inspired man with love—love for his fellow beings and love of the beautiful—could not be the same Creator who framed that irredeemably cruel principle observable throughout nature, *i.e.*, the survival of the fittest; the preying of the stronger on the weaker—of the tiger on the feebler beasts of the jungle; the eagle on the smaller birds of the air; the wolf on the sheep; the shark on the poor, defenceless fish, and so on; neither could He be the Creator that deals in diseases—foul and filthy diseases, common, not only to all divisions of the human species, but to quadrupeds, birds, fish, and even flora; that brings into existence cripples and idiots, the blind, the deaf and dumb; and watches with passive inertness the most acute sufferings, not only of adults, but of sinless children and all manner of helpless animals. No! It is impossible to conceive that such incompatibilities can be the work of one Creator. But, supposing, for the sake of argument, we may admit the possibility of only one Creator, we cannot concede that this Creator is at the same time both omnipotent and merciful. My own belief, which is merely based on common sense and observation, is that this earth was created by many Forces—that everything that makes for man's welfare is due to Benevolent Forces; and that everything that tends to his detriment is due to antagonistic Malevolent Forces; and that the Malevolent Forces exist for the very simple reason that the Benevolent Forces are not sufficiently powerful to destroy them.

These Malevolent Forces, then—the originators of all evil—created werwolves; and the property of lycanthropy becoming in many cases hereditary, there were families that could look back upon countless generations possessed of it. But lycanthropy did not remain in the exclusive possession of a few families; the bestowal of it continued long after its original creation, and I doubt if this bestowal has, even now, become entirely a thing of the past. There are still a few regions—desolate and isolated regions in Europe (in Russia, Scandinavia, and even France), to say nothing of Asia, Africa and America, Australasia and Polynesia—which are unquestionably the haunts of Vagrarians, Barrowvians, and other kinds of undesirable Elementals, and it is quite possible that, through the agency of these spirits, the property of lycanthropy might be acquired by those who have learned in solitude how to commune with them.

I have already referred to the werwolf as an anomaly, and for its designation I do not think I could have chosen a more suitable term. Though its movements and actions are physical—for what could be more material than the act of devouring flesh and blood?—the actual process of the metamorphosis savours of the superphysical; whilst to still further strengthen its relationship with the latter, its appearance is sometimes half man and half wolf, which is certainly more than suggestive of the semi-human and by no means uncommon type of Elemental. Its inconsistency, too, which is a striking characteristic of all psychic phenomena, is also suggestive of the superphysical; and there is certainly neither consistency as to the nature of the metamorphosis—which is sometimes brought about at will and sometimes entirely controlled by the hour of day, or by the seasons—nor as to the outward form of the werwolf, which is sometimes merely that of a wolf, and sometimes partly wolf and partly human; nor as to its shape at the moment of death, when in some cases there is metamorphosis, whilst in other cases there is no metamorphosis. Nor is this inconsistency only characteristic of the movements, actions, and shape of the werwolf. It is also characteristic of it psychologically. When the metamorphosis is involuntary, and is enforced by agencies over which the subject has no control, the werwolf, though filled with all the passions characteristic of a beast of prey, when a wolf, is not of necessity cruel and savage when a human being, that is to say, before the transmutations take place. There are many instances of such werwolves being, as people, affectionate and kindly disposed. On the other hand, in some cases of involuntary metamorphosis, and in the majority of cases of voluntary metamorphosis—that is to say, when the transmutation is compassed by means of magic—the werwolf, as a person, is evilly disposed, and as a wolf shows a distinct blending of the beast with the passions, subtle ingenuity, and reasoning powers of the human being. From this it is obvious, then, that the werwolf is a hybrid of the material and immaterial—of man and Elemental, known and Unknown. The latter term does not, of course, meet with acceptance at the hands of the Rationalists, who profess to believe that all phenomena can be explained by perfectly natural causes. They suggest that belief in the werwolf (as indeed in all other forms of lycanthropy) is traceable to the craving for blood which is innate in certain natures and is sometimes accompanied by hallucination, the subject genuinely believing himself to be a wolf (or whatever beast of prey is most common in the district), and, in imitation of that animal's habits, committing acts of devastation at night, selecting his victims principally from among women and children—those, in fact, who are too feeble to resist him.

Often, however, say these Rationalists, there is no suggestion of hallucination, the question resolving itself into one of vulgar trickery. The anthropophagi, unable to suppress their appetite for human food, taking advantage of the general awe in which the wolf is held by their neighbours, dress themselves up in the skins of that beast, and prowling about lonely, isolated spots at night, pounce upon those people they can most easily overpower. Rumours (most probably started by the murderers themselves) speedily get in circulation that the mangled and half-eaten remains of the villagers are attributable to creatures, half human and half wolf, that have been seen gliding about certain places after dark. The simple country-folk, among whom superstitions are rife, are only too ready to give credence to such reports; the existence of the monsters becomes an established thing, whilst the localities that harbour them are regarded with horror, and looked upon as the happy hunting ground of every imaginable occult power of evil.

Now, although such an explanation of werwolves might be applicable in certain districts of West Africa, where the native population is excessively bloodthirsty and ignorant, it could not for one moment be applied to werwolfery in Germany, France, or Scandinavia, where the peasantry are, generally speaking, kindly and intelligent people, whom one could certainly accuse neither of being sanguinary nor of possessing any natural taste for cannibalism.

The rationalist view can therefore only be said to be feasible in certain limited spheres, outside of which it is grotesque and ridiculous.

Now a question that has occurred to me, and which, I fancy, may give rise to some interesting speculation, is, whether some of the werwolves stated to have been seen may not have been some peculiar type of phantasm. I make this suggestion because I have seen several sub-human and sub-animal occult phenomena in England, and have, too, met other people who have had similar experiences.

With our limited knowledge of the Unknown it is, of course, impossible to be arbitrary as to the class of spirits to which such phenomena belong. They may be Vice Elementals, *i.e.*, spirits that have never inhabited any material body, whether human or animal, and which are wholly inimical to man's progress—such spirits assume an infinite number of shapes, agreeable and otherwise; or they may be phantasms of dead human beings—vicious and carnal-minded people, idiots, and imbecile epileptics. It is an old belief that the souls of cataleptic and epileptic people, during the body's unconsciousness, adjourned temporarily to animals, and it is therefore only in keeping with such a view to suggest that on the deaths of such people their spirits take permanently the form of animals. This would account for the fact that places where cataleptics and idiots have died are often haunted by semi and by wholly animal types of phantasms.

According to Paracelsus Man has in him two spirits—an animal spirit and a human spirit—and that in after life he appears in the shape of whichever of these two spirits he has allowed to dominate him. If, for example, he has obeyed the spirit that prompts him to be sober and temperate, then his phantasm resembles a man; but on the other hand, if he has given way to his carnal and bestial cravings, then his phantasm is earthbound, in the guise of some terrifying and repellent animal—maybe a wolf, bear, dog, or cat—all of which shapes are far from uncommon in psychic manifestations.

This view has been held either *in toto*, or with certain reservations, by many other writers on the subject, and I, too, in a great measure endorse it—its pronouncement of a limit to man's phantasms being, perhaps, the only important point to which I cannot accede. My own view is that so complex a creature as man—complex both physically and psychologically—may have a representative spirit for each of his personalities. Hence on man's physical dissolution there may emanate from him a host of phantasms, each with a shape most fitting the personality it represents. And what more thoroughly representative of cruelty, savageness, and treachery than a wolf, or even something partly lupine! Therefore, as I have suggested elsewhere, in some instances, but emphatically not in all, what were thought to have been werwolves may only have been phantasms of the dead, or Elementals.

CHAPTER II

# Werwolf Metamorphosis Compared with Other Branches of Lycanthropy

THE WOLF IS not the only animal whose shape, it is stated, man may possess the power of assuming; and it may be of some interest to inquire briefly into the varying branches of lycanthropy, comparing them with the one already under discussion.

In Orissa, the power of metamorphosing into a tiger is asserted by the Kandhs to be hereditary, and also to be acquired through the practice of magic; many who have travelled in this country have assured me that there is a very great amount of truth in this assertion; and that although there are, without doubt, a number of impostors among those designated wer-tigers, there are most certainly many who are genuine.

As with the werwolf, so with the wer-tiger, the metamorphosis is usually dependent on the hour of the day, and generally occurs cotemporaneous with the setting of the sun.

But the lycanthropy of the wer-tiger differs from that of the werwolf inasmuch as there is a definite god or spirit, in the shape of a tiger, that is directly responsible for the bestowal of the property. This tiger deity is looked upon and worshipped as a totem or national deity—that is to say, as a divine being that has the welfare of the Kandh nation especially at heart. It is communed with at home, but more particularly in the wild dreariness of the jungle, where, on the condition that the prayers of its devotees are sufficiently concentrated and in earnest, it confers—as an honour and privilege—the power of transmutation into its own shape. Some idea of its appearance may perhaps be gathered from the following description of it given me by a Mr. K——, whose name I see in the list of passengers reported "missing" in the deplorable disaster to the "Titanic."

"Anxious to see," Mr. K—— stated, "if there was anything of truth in the alleged materialization of the tiger totem to those supplicating it, I went one evening to a spot in the jungle—some two or three miles from the village—where I had been informed the manifestations took place. As the jungle was universally held to be haunted I met no one; and in spite of my dread of the snakes, big cats, wild boars, scorpions, and other poisonous vermin with which the place was swarming, arrived without mishap at the place that had been so carefully described to me—a circular clearing of about twenty feet in diameter, surrounded on all sides by rank grass of a prodigious height, trolsee shrubs, kulpa and tamarind-trees. Quickly concealing myself, I waited the coming of the would-be tiger-man.

"He was hardly more than a boy—slim and almost feminine—and came gallivanting along the narrow path through the brushwood, like some careless, high-spirited, brown-skinned hoyden.

"The moment he reached the edge of the mystic circle, however, his behaviour changed; the light of laughter died from his eyes, his lips straightened, his limbs stiffened, and his whole demeanour became one of respect and humility.

"Advancing with bare head and feet some three or so feet into the clearing, he knelt down, and, touching the ground three times in succession with his forehead, looked up at a giant kulpa-tree opposite him, chanting as he did so some weird and monotonous refrain, the meaning of which was unintelligible to me. Up to then it had been light—the sky, like all Indian skies at that season, one blaze of moonbeams and stars; but now it gradually grew dark. An unnatural, awe-inspiring shade seemed to swoop down from the far distant mountains and to hush into breathless silence everything it touched. Not a bird sang, not an insect ticked, not a leaf stirred. One might have said all nature slept, had it not been for an uncomfortable sensation that the silence was but the silence of intense expectation—merely the prelude to some unpleasant revelation that was to follow. At this juncture my feelings were certainly novel—entirely different from any I had hitherto experienced.

"I had not believed in the supernatural, and had had absolutely no apprehensions of coming across anything of a ghostly character—all my fears had been of malicious natives and tigers; they now, however, changed, and I was confronted with a dread of what I could not understand and could not analyse—of something that suggested an appearance, alarming on account of its very vagueness.

"The pulsations of my heart became irregular, I grew faint and sick, and painfully susceptible to a sensation of excessive coldness, which instinct told me was quite independent of any actual change in the atmosphere.

"I made several attempts to remove my gaze from the kulpa-tree, which intuition told me would be the spot where the something, whatever it was, that was going to happen would manifest itself. My eyes, however, refused to obey, and I was obliged to keep them steadily fixed on this spot, which grew more and more gloomy. All of a sudden the silence was broken, and a cry, half human and half animal, but horribly ominous, sounding at first faint and distant, speedily grew louder and louder. Soon I heard footsteps, the footsteps of something running towards us and covering the ground with huge, light strides. Nearer and nearer it came, till, with a sudden spring, it burst into view—the giant reeds and trolsees were dashed aside, and I saw standing in front of the kulpa-tree a vertical column of crimson light of perhaps seven feet in height and one or so in width. A column—only a column, though the suggestion conveyed to me by the column was nasty—nasty with a nastiness that baffles description. I looked at the native, and the expression in his eyes and mouth assured me he saw more—a very great deal more. For some seconds he only gasped; then, by degrees, the rolling of his eyes and twitching of his lips ceased. He stretched out a hand and made some sign on the ground. Then he produced a string of beads, and after placing it over the scratchings he had made on the soil, jerked out some strange incantation in a voice that thickened and quivered with terror. I then saw a stream of red light steal from the base of the column and dart like forked lightning to the beads, which instantly shone a luminous red. The native now picked them up, and, putting them round his neck, clapped the palms of his hands vigorously together, uttering as he did so a succession of shrill cries, that gradually became more and more animal in tone, and finally ended in a roar that converted every particle of blood in my veins into ice. The crimson colour now abruptly vanished—whither it went I know not—the shade that had been veiling the jungle was dissipated, and in the burst of brilliant moonlight that succeeded I saw, peering up at me, from the spot where the native had lain, the yellow, glittering, malevolent eyes, not of a man, but a tiger—a tiger thirsting for human blood. The shock was so great that for a second or two I was paralysed, and could only stare back at the thing in fascinated helplessness. Then a big bird close at hand screeched, and some small quadruped flew past me terrified; and with these awakenings of nature all my faculties revived, and I simply jumped on my feet and—fled!

"Some fifty yards ahead of me, and showing their tops well above the moon-kissed reeds and bushes, were two trees—a tamarind and a kulpa briksha. God knows why I decided on the latter! Probably through a mere fluke, for I hadn't the remotest idea which of the trees offered the best facilities to a poor climber. My mind once made up, there was no time to alter. The wer-tiger was already terribly close behind. I could gauge its distance by the patter of its feet—apparently the metamorphosis had only been in part—and by the steadily intensifying purr, purr; so unmistakably interpretative of the brute's utter satisfaction in its power to overtake me, as well as at the prospect of so good a meal. I was just thirteen stone, seemingly a most unlucky number even in weight! Had the tiger wanted, I am sure he could have caught me at once, but I fancy it wished to play with me a little first—to let me think I was going to escape, and then, when it had got all the amusement possible out of me, just to give a little sprint and haul me over. Perhaps it was my anger at such undignified treatment of the human race that gave a kind of sting to my running, for I certainly got over the ground at twice the speed I had ever done before, or ever thought myself capable of doing. At times my limbs were on the verge of mutiny, but I forced them onward, and though my lungs seemed bursting, I never paused. At last a clearing was reached and the kulpa-tree stood fully revealed. I glanced at once at the trunk. The lowest branch of any size was some eight feet from the ground. . . . Could I reach it? Summoning up all my efforts for this final, and in all probability fatal, rush, I hurled myself forward. There was a low exultant roar, a soft, almost feminine purr, and a long hairy paw, with black, gleaming claws shot past my cheek. I gave a great gasp of anguish, and with all the pent-up force of despair clutched at the branch overhead. My finger-tips just curled over it; I tightened them, but, at the most, it was a very feeble, puny grasp, and totally insufficient to enable me to swing my body out of reach of the tiger. I immediately gave myself up as lost, and was endeavouring to reconcile myself to the idea of being slowly chewed alive, when an extraordinary thing happened. The wer-tiger gave a low growl of terror and, bounding away, was speedily lost in the jungle. Fearing it might return, I waited for some time in the tree, and then, as there were no signs of it, descended, and very cautiously made my way back to the village.

"That night an entire family, father, mother, son, and daughter, were murdered, and their mutilated and half-eaten bodies were discovered on the floor of their hut in the morning. Evidence pointed to their having been killed by a tiger; and as they had been the sworn enemies of the young man whose metamorphosis I had witnessed, it was not difficult to guess at the identity of their destroyer.

"I related my adventure to one of the chief people, and he informed me he knew that particular kulpa-tree well. 'You undoubtedly owe your salvation to having touched it,' he said. 'The original kulpa, which now stands in the first heaven, is said to have been one of the fourteen remarkable things turned up by the churning of the ocean by the gods and demons; and the name of Ram and his consort Seeter are written on the silvery trunks of all its earthly descendants. If once you touch any portion of a kulpa briksha tree, you are quite safe from any animal—that is why the wer-tiger snarled and ran away! But take my advice, sahib, and leave the village.'

"I did so, and on the way to my home in the hills visited the tree. There, sure enough, plainly visible on the silvery surface in the twilight, was the name of the incarnation of Vishnu, written in Sanskrit characters, and apparently by some supernatural hand; that is to say, there was a softness in the impression, as if the finger of some supernatural being had traced the characters. I did not want any further proofs—I had had enough; and taking good care to see my gun was loaded, I hurried off. Nor have I ever ventured into that neighbourhood since."

Mr. K——, continuing, informed me that from what he had been told by his friend in the Kandh village, he concluded that only those who had been initiated into the full rites of magic in their early youth could see the totem in its full state of materialization, *i.e.*, an enormous tiger—half man and half beast. To those who were in some degree clairvoyant it would appear as it had appeared to him, a mere column of crimson light (crimson on account of its association with Black Magic); whilst to those who were not in any way clairvoyant it would remain entirely invisible. The young Kandh had prayed for the property of lycanthropy solely as a means of revenge on those whom he imagined had wronged him; and as a wer-tiger he was able to destroy them in the most cruel manner possible. The property when once acquired, however, could never be cast off, and the young man would, willy-nilly, undergo transmutation every night, and in all probability continue killing and eating people till some one plucked up the courage—for wer-tigers were not only dreaded, but held in the greatest awe—to shoot him.

There are certain tribes in India known to be adepts in Occultism, and therefore one is not surprised to find lycanthropy linked with the mysterious jugglery, etherical projection, and other psychic feats accomplished by these tribesmen. The wer-tiger is not confined to the Kandhs: it is met with in Malaysia, in the gorgeous tropical forests of Java and Sumatra, where it is feared more than anything on earth by the gentle and intelligent natives; and, if rumour be true, in the great, lone mountains and dense jungles, and along the hot, unhealthy river-banks of New Guinea.

In Arawak, it gives place to the wer-jaguar; in Ashangoland, and many parts of West Africa, to the wer-leopard. Of course, there are cases of charlatanism in lycanthropy as in medicine, politics, palmistry, and in every other science. But most, if not all, of these cases of sham lycanthropy seem to come from West Africa, where leopard societies are from time to time formed by young savages unable to restrain their craving for cannibalism. These human vampires dress up in leopard-skins, and stealing stealthily through the woods at night, attack stray pedestrians or isolated households. After killing their victims, they cut off any portions of the body—usually the breasts and thighs—they fancy most for eating, and then mutilate the rest with the signia of their society, *i.e.*, long and deep scratchings, which are made either with the claws of a leopard or some other beast, or with sharp iron nails. Whole districts are often put in a state of panic by these marauders, who, retiring to their retreat in the heart of some little known, vast, and almost impenetrable forest, successfully defy capture. But the fact of there being pseudo-wer-leopards by no means disposes of the fact that there are genuine ones, any more than the fact that there are charlatan palmists precludes the possibility of there being *bona fide* palmists; and I am inclined to believe lycanthropy exists in certain parts of West Africa (*i.e.*, where primitive conditions are most in evidence), although not, perhaps, to the same extent as it does in Asia and Europe. I do not think the negro's relationship to the Occult Forces is quite the same as that of other races. He is often clairvoyant and clairaudiant, and always very much in awe of the superphysical; but it is rarely he can ever claim close intimacy with it—not close enough, at all events, to be the recipient of its special gifts.

In werwolfery there is no "totem." The property of metamorphosis, in this branch of lycanthropy, is not deemed the gift of a national deity, but either of the Occult Powers in general or of some particular local phantasm. In other branches of lycanthropy, viz., that of the wer-tiger and wer-leopard—I am doubtful about the wer-jaguar—the property of transmutation is said to be conferred solely by the god, or a god, of the tribe.

But although these various properties of lycanthropy are apparently derived from different sources, the difference is only in outward form; and I have no hesitation in saying that the occult power from which all lycanthropy proceeds, whether in the form of a wolf, tiger, leopard, or any other beast, is in reality the same species of Elemental.[1] But whether a Vagrarian, Vice, or some other Elemental, I cannot possibly say.

I have stated that I am doubtful as to whether totemism exists in Arawak. The truth is, with regard to this question, I am in receipt of somewhat conflicting testimony. Some say that the natives have as their god a deity in the form of a jaguar, to whom they pray for vengeance on their foes and for the property of lycanthropy; which property (*vide* the case of the Kandhs) would give them the additional pleasure of executing vengeance in their own person. On the other hand, I have heard that the form of a jaguar is the form most commonly assumed by spirits in Arawak, particularly by those invoked at séances. Hence it is extremely difficult to arrive at the truth. From the corroborating testimony of various people, however, I conclude that whereas among the Kandhs and West African negroes the property of lycanthropy (unless, of course, hereditary) is rarely conferred on females, or on anyone younger than sixteen, in Arawak and Malaysia it is awarded regardless of sex or age.

Some years ago there was current, among certain tribes of the natives in Arawak, a story to this effect:—

---

1 A spirit that has never inhabited any material body. Elementals are a genus of a large order, and include innumerable species.

A Dutch trader, of the name of Van Hielen, was visiting for purely business purposes an Indian settlement in a very remote part of the colony. Roaming about the village one evening, he came to a hut standing alone on the outskirts of one of those dense forests that are so characteristic of Arawak. Van Hielen paused, and was marvelling how anyone could choose to live in so outlandish and lonely a spot, when a shrill scream, followed by a series of violent guttural ejaculations, came from the interior of the building, and the next moment a little boy—some seven or eight years of age—rushed out of the house, pursued by a prodigiously fat woman, who whacked him soundly across the shoulders with a knotted club and then halted for want of breath. Van Hielen, who was well versed in the native language, politely asked her what the boy had done to deserve so severe a chastisement.

"Done!" the woman replied, opening her beady little eyes to their full extent; "why, he's not done anything—that's why I beat him—he's incorrigibly idle. He and his sister spend all their time amid the trees yonder conversing with the bad spirits. They learned that trick from Guska, with the evil eye. She has bewitched them. She was shot to death with arrows in the market-place last year, and my only regret is that she wasn't put out of the way ten years sooner. Ah! there's that wicked girl Yarakna—she's been hiding from me all the day. I must punish her, too!" and before Van Hielen could speak the indignant parent waddled off—with surprising swiftness for one of her vast proportions—and reappeared dragging by the wrist an elfish-looking girl of about ten. She gave the urchin one blow, and was about to give her another, when Van Hielen, whose heart was particularly tender where children were concerned, interfered, and by dint of bribery persuaded her to desist. She retired indoors, and Van Hielen found himself alone with the child.

"May the spirit of the woods for ever be your friend!" the maiden said. "But for you my poor back would have been beaten to a tonka bean. My brother and I have suffered enough at the hands of the old woman—we'll suffer no more."

"What will you do then?" Van Hielen asked, shocked at the revengeful expression that marred the otherwise pretty features of the child. "Remember, she is your mother, and has every right to expect you to be obedient and industrious."

"She is not our mother!" the girl answered. "Our mother is the spirit of the woods. We work for her—not for this old woman, and in return she tells us tales and amuses us."

"You work for her!" Van Hielen said in amazement. "What do you mean?"

The child smiled—the ignorance of the white man tickled her. "We gather aloes for medicine for her sick children; the core of the lechugilla for their food, yucca leaves for plumes for their heads, and scarlet panicles of the *Fouquiera splendens* for their clothes. My brother and I will go to her to-night when the old woman is sleeping. Where? Ah! we do not tell anyone that. Do we see her? The spirit of the woods, you mean? Yes, we see her, but it is not every one who can see her—only those who have sight like ours. But I must go now—my brother is calling me."

Van Hielen could hear nothing; though he did not doubt, from the child's behaviour, that she had been called. She ran merrily away, and he watched her black head disappear in the thick undergrowth facing him. Van Hielen's curiosity was roused. What the child had said impressed him deeply; and against his saner judgment he resolved to secrete himself near the hut and watch. After it had been dusk some time, and all sounds had ceased, he saw the two children emerge from the hut, and, tiptoeing softly towards the trees, fall on their hands and knees and crawl along a tiny, deviating path. Hardly knowing what he was doing, but impelled by a force he could not resist, Van Hielen followed them. It was a delicious night—at that time of year every night in Arawak is delicious—and Van Hielen, who was very simple in his love of nature, imbibed delight through every pore in his body. As he trod gently along, pushing first this branch and then that out of the way, and stooping down to half his height to creep under a formidable bramble, countless voices from animal land fell on his ears. From a glimmering patch of water, away on his left, came the trump of a bull-frog and the wail of the whip-poor-will; a monkey chattered, a parrot screeched, whilst a shrill cry of terror, accompanied by a savage growl, plainly told of the surprise and slaughter of some defenceless animal by one of the many big beasts of prey that made every tree their lurking place.

On any other occasion Van Hielen would have thought twice before embarking on such an expedition; but that night he seemed to be labouring under some charm which had lulled to sleep all sense of insecurity. It was true he was armed, but of what avail is a rifle against the unexpected spring of a jaguar or leopard—from a bough some ten or twenty feet directly over one's head—or the sudden lunge of a boa constrictor!

At first, the path wound its way through a dense chapparal consisting of the various shrubs and plants rarely to be met with in other parts of Arawak, namely, acacias, aloes, lechuguillas, and the *Fouquiera splendens*. But after a short time this kind of vegetation was succeeded by something far more imposing—by dense masses of trees, many of them at the least one hundred and fifty feet in height: the mora, which from a distance appears like a hillock clothed with the brightest vegetation; the ayucari, or red cedar; and the cuamara, laden with tonka beans. So thick was their foliage overhead that one by one Van Hielen watched the stars disappear; and the path ahead of him darkened till it was as much as he could do to grope along. Still he was not afraid. The thought of that elfish little maiden with the luminous eyes crawling along in front of him inspired him with extraordinary confidence and he plunged on, anxious only to catch another glimpse of her and see the play out. Once his progress was interrupted by something hot and leathery, that pushed him nearly off his feet and puffed rudely in his face. It was on the tip of his tongue to give vent to his ruffled feelings in forcible language, but the knowledge that this would assuredly warn the children of his proximity kept him quiet, and he contented himself with striking a vigorous blow. There was a loud snort, a crashing and breaking of brushwood, and the thing, whatever it was, rushed away. Another time he stumbled over a snake which was gliding from one side of the path to the other. The creature hissed, and Van Hielen, giving himself up for lost, jumped for all he was worth. As luck would have it the snake missed, and Van Hielen, escaping with nothing more serious than a few scratches and a bump or two, was able to continue his course. After long gropings the path at length came to an end, the trees cleared, and Van Hielen saw before him a pool, radiantly illuminated by the moon, and in the very centre—an immense Victoria Regia water-lily.

Though accustomed to the fine species of this plant in Guiana—which is the home of the Victoria Regia—Van Hielen was doubtful if he had ever before beheld such a magnificent specimen. The silvery moonlight, falling on its white and pink petals, threw into relief all the exquisite delicacy of their composition, and gave to them a glow which could only have been rivalled in Elysium. Indeed, the whole scene, enhanced by the glamour of the hour and the sweet scent of plants and flowers, was so reminiscent of fairyland that Van Hielen—enraptured beyond description—stood and gazed in open-mouthed ecstasy.

Then his eyes fell on the children and he noiselessly slipped back under cover of a tree.

Hand in hand the boy and girl advanced to the water's edge, and kneeling, commenced to recite some strange incantation, which Van Hielen tried in vain to interpret. Sometimes their voices reached a high, plaintive key; sometimes they sank to a low murmur, strangely musical, and strangely suggestive of the babbling of brook water over stones and pebbles. When they had finished their incantation, they got up, and running to some bushes, returned in a few seconds with their arms full of flowers, which they threw with great dexterity on to the leaves of the giant lily. With their faces still turned to the water they remained standing, side by side, whilst a silence—deep and impressive, and shared, so it appeared to Van Hielen, by all nature—fell upon them.

A cold current of air, rising apparently from the pool, blew across the opening, and sweeping past Van Hielen, set all the leaves in motion. It rustled on till its echoes gradually ceased, and all was still again. It now seemed to Van Hielen that the character of everything around underwent a subtle change; and the feeling that every object around him was indulging in a hearty laugh at his expense intensified with every breath he drew. For the first time Van Hielen was afraid. He could not define the cause of his fear—but that only made his fear the more acute. He was frightened of the wind and darkness, and of something more than the wind and darkness—something concealed in—something cloaked by the wind and darkness. Even the atmosphere had altered—it, too, was making game of him. It distorted his vision. The things he saw around him were no longer stationary—they moved. They twirled and twisted themselves into all sorts of grotesque and fanciful attitudes; grew large, then small; nearer and then more distant. The plot of ground in front of which the children knelt played all manner of pranks—pranks Van Hielen did not at all like. It moved round and round—faster and faster, until it eventually became a whirlpool; which suddenly reversed and assumed the appearance of a pyramid revolving on its apex. Quicker and quicker it spun round—closer and closer it drew; until, without warning, it suddenly stopped and disappeared; whilst its place was taken by an oddly shaped bulge in the ground, which, swaying backward and forward, increased and increased in stature, till it attained the height of some seven or eight feet. Van Hielen could not compare this with anything he had ever seen. It was monstrous but shapeless—a mere mass of irregular lumps, a dull leadish white, and vibrating horribly in the moonlight. He thought of the children; but where they had stood he saw only two greenish-yellow spheres that, twirling round and round, suddenly approached him. As he started back to escape them, all was again changed. The lumpy figure had vanished, the atmosphere cleared, and everything was absolutely normal. There were now, however, solid grounds for fear. Advancing on him with flashing eyes and scintillating teeth were two vividly marked jaguars—a male and female. Van Hielen, usually calm and collected in the face of danger, on this occasion lost his presence of mind: his gun dropped from his hands, his knees quivered, and, helpless and inert, he reeled against the tree under which he had been standing. The jaguars—which seemed to be unusually savage even for jaguars—prepared to spring, and Van Hielen, certain his hour had come, was about to close his eyes and resign himself to his fate, when the female brute, although the bigger and more formidable, hesitated—thrust its dark, handsomely spotted head almost in its victim's face, and then, lashing its companion sharply with its tail, swerved aside and was off like a dart.

It took Van Hielen some minutes to realize his escape, and then, more in a dream than awake, he mechanically shouldered his rifle and slowly followed in the beasts' wake.

An hour's walking brought him to the end of the forest. The dawn was breaking, and the track leading to the settlement was just beginning to exhibit the mellowing influence of the first rays of the sun. There was an exhilarating freshness in the air that made Van Hielen keenly sensitive to the ambitious demands of a newly awakened stomach. Opposite him was the hut of the old woman, the entrance somewhat clumsily blocked with a makeshift door. As Van Hielen looked at it curiously, wondering if the woman was in the habit of barricading it in this fashion on account of her proximity to the forest, sounds greeted him from within.

Stepping lightly up to the hut, Van Hielen listened attentively. Some big animal—a hound most probably—was gnawing a bone—crunch, crunch, crunch!

Van Hielen moved away, but hadn't gone very far before an indefinable something made him turn back. That crunching, was it a dog or was it——? His heart turned sick within him at the bare thought. Again he listened at the threshold, and again he heard the sounds—gnaw, gnaw, gnaw—crunch, crunch, crunch! He rapped at first gently, and then loudly, ever so loudly.

The gnawing at once stopped, but no one answered him. Then he called—once, twice, thrice: there was no reply. Assured now there was something amiss, he gripped his rifle, and putting his shoulder to the door, burst it open. A flood of daylight rushed in, and he saw before him on the floor the mutilated and half-eaten remains of a woman, and—did his eyes deceive him or did he see?—crouching in a corner all ready to spring, two magnificent jaguars. Van Hielen raised his rifle, but—in less than a second—it fell from his grasp.

Towards him, from the same spot—their small mouths and slender hands smeared with blood—ran Yarakna and her brother.

# CHAPTER III
# The Spirits of Werwolves

**IT SEEMS THAT** there is a disposition in certain minds to associate lycanthropy with the doctrine of the transmigration of souls. A brief examination of the latter will, however, suffice to show there is very little analogy between the two.

Transmigration of souls, a metempsychosis, deals solely with the passing of the soul after death into another mortal form. Lycanthropy confines itself to the metamorphosis of physical man to animal form only during man's physical lifetime.

Metempsychosis is a change of condition dependent on the principle of evolution (*i.e.* evolution upward and retrogressive). Lycanthropy is a change of condition relative to a property, entirely independent of evolution. The one is wholly determined by man's spiritual state at the time of his physical dissolution; the other is simply a faculty of sense, either handed down to man by his forefathers or acquired by man, during his lifetime, through the knowledge and practice of magic.

There are absolutely no grounds, other than purely hypothetical ones, for supposing a werwolf to be a reincarnation; but on the other hand there is reason to believe that the wolf personality of the werwolf, at the latter's physical dissolution, remains earthbound in the form of a lupine phantasm. So that although there is nothing to associate lycanthropy with metempsychosis, there is, at all events, something in common between lycanthropy and animism. Animism, be it understood, holds that every living thing, whether man, beast, reptile, insect, or vegetable, has a representative spirit.

As an example of a lupine phantasm representing the personality of the werwolf, I will quote a case, reported to me some years ago as having occurred in Estonia, on the shores of the Baltic. A gentleman and his sister, whom I will call Stanislaus and Anno D'Adhemar, were invited to spend a few weeks with their old friends, the Baron and Baroness Von A——, at their country home in Estonia. On the day arranged, they set out for their friends' house, and alighting at a little station, within twenty miles of their destination, were met by the Baron's droshky. It was one of those exquisite evenings—a night light without moon, a day shady without clouds—peculiar to that clime. Indeed, it seemed as if the last glow of the evening and the first grey of the morning had melted together, and as if all the luminaries of the sky merely rested their beams without withdrawing them. To Stanislaus and Anno, jaded with the wear and tear of life in a big city, the calm and quiet of the country-side was most refreshing, and they heaved great sighs of contentment as they leaned far back amid the luxurious upholstery of the carriage, and drew in deep breaths of the smokeless, pure, scented air. Their surroundings modelled their thoughts. Instead of discussing monetary matters, which had so long been uppermost in their minds, they discoursed on the wonderful economy of happiness in a world full of toil and struggle; the fewer the joys, they argued, the higher the enjoyment, till the last and highest joy of all, true peace of mind, *i.e.*, content, was the one joy found to contain every other joy. Occasionally they paused to remark on the brilliant lustre of the stars, and, not infrequently, alluded to the Creator's graciousness in allowing them to behold such beauty. Occasionally, too, they would break off in the midst of their conversation to listen to the plaintive utterings of some night bird or the shrill cry of a startled hare. The rate at which they were progressing—for the horses were young and fresh—speedily brought them to an end of the open country, and they found themselves suddenly immersed in the deepening gloom of a dense and extensive forest of pines. The track now was not quite so smooth; here and there were big ruts, and Stanislaus and his sister were subjected to such a vigorous bumping that they had to hold on to the sides of the droshky, and to one another. In the altered conditions of their travel, conversation was well-nigh impossible. The little they attempted was unceremoniously jerked out of them, and the nature of it—I am loath to admit—had somewhat deteriorated. It had, in fact, in accordance with their surroundings, undergone a considerable change.

"What a vile road!" Stanislaus exclaimed, clutching the side of the droshky with both hands to save himself from being precipitated into space.

"Yes—isn't—it?" gasped Anno, as she lunged forward, and in a vain attempt to regain her seat fell on their handbag, which gave an ominous squish. "I declare there—there—will be—nothing left of me—by the—by the time we get there. Oh dear! Whatever shall I do?

Wherever have you got to, Stanislaus?"

The upper half of Stanislaus was nowhere to be seen! His lower half, however, was discovered by his sister convulsively pressed against the side of the droshky. In another moment this, too, would undoubtedly have disappeared, and the lower extremities would have gone in pursuit of the upper, had not Anno with admirable presence of mind effected a rescue. She tugged at her brother's coat-tails in the very nick of time, with the result that his whole body once again hove into view.

Just then a bird sang its final song before retiring for the night, and Stanislaus, hot and trembling all over, shouted out: "What a hideous noise! I declare it quite frightened me"; whilst Anno shuddered and put her fingers in her ears. They once more abused the road; then the trees. "Great ugly things," they said; "they shut out all the light." And then they abused the driver for not looking out where he was going, and finally they began to abuse one another. Anno abused Stanislaus, because he had disarranged her hat and hair, and Stanislaus, Anno, because he couldn't hear all she said, and because what he did hear was silly. Then the Stygian darkness of the great pines grew; and the silence of wonder fell on the two quarrellers. On, on, on rolled the droshky, a monotonous rumble, rumble, that sounded very loud amid the intense hush that had suddenly fallen on the forest. Stanislaus and Anno grew drowsy; the cold night air, crowning their exertions of the day, induced sleep, and they were soon very much in the land of nods: Stanislaus with his head thrust back as far as it would go, and Anno with her head leaning slightly forward and her chin deeply rooted in the silvery recesses of her rich fur coat.

The driver stopped for a moment. He had to attend to his lights, which, he reflected, were behaving in rather an odd manner. Then, scratching his head thoughtfully, he cracked his whip and drove hurriedly on. Once again, rumble, rumble, rumble; and no other sounds but far away echoes and the gentle cooing of a soft night breeze through the forked and ragged branches of the sad and stately pines. On, on, on, the light uncertain and the horses brisk. Suddenly the driver hears something—he strains his ears to catch the meaning of the sounds—a peculiar, quick patter, patter—coming from far away in the droshky's wake. There is something—he can't exactly tell what—in those sounds he doesn't like; they are human, and yet not human; they may proceed from some one running—some one tall and lithe, with an unusually long stride. They may—and he casts a shuddering look over his shoulder as the thought strikes him—they may be nothing human—they may be the patter of a wolf! A huge, gaunt, hungry wolf! an abnormally big wolf! a wolf with a gallop like that of a horse! The driver was new to these parts; he had but lately come from the Baron's establishment in St. Petersburg. He had never been in this wood after dark, and he had never seen a wolf save in the Zoological Gardens. The atmosphere now began to sharpen. From being merely cold it became positively icy, and muttering, "I never felt anything like this in St. Petersburg," the driver shrank into the depths of his furs, and tried to settle himself more comfortably in his seat. The horses, too, four in number, were strangers in Estonia, the Baron having only recently paid a heavy price for them in Nava on account of their beauty. Not that they were merely handsome;

despite their small and graceful build, and the glossy sleekness of their coats, they were both strong and spirited, and could cover twenty-five versts without a pause. But now they, too, heard the sounds—there was no doubt of that—and felt the cold. At first they shivered, then whined, and then came to an abrupt halt; and then, without the slightest warning, tore the shifting tag and rag tight around them, and bounding forward, were off like the wind. Then, away in their rear, and plainly audible above the thunder of their hoofs, came a moaning, snarling, drawn-out cry, which was almost instantly repeated, not once, but again and again.

Stanislaus and Anno, who had been rudely awakened from their slumbers by the unusual behaviour of the horses, were now on the *qui vive*.

"Good heavens! What's that?" they cried in chorus.

"What's that, coachman?" shrieked Anno, digging the shivering driver in the back.

"Volki, mistress, volki!" was the reply, and on flew the droshky faster, faster, faster!

To Stanislaus and Anno the word "wolves" came as a stunning shock. All the tales they had ever heard of these ferocious beasts crowded their minds at once. Wolves! was it possible that those dreadful bogies of their childhood—those grim and awful creatures, grotesquely but none the less vividly portrayed in their imagination by horror-loving nurses—were actually close at hand! Supposing the brutes caught them, who would be eaten first? Anno, Stanislaus, or the driver? Would they devour them with their clothes on? If not, how would they get them off? Then, filled with morbid curiosity, they strained their ears and listened. Again—this time nearer, much nearer—came that cry, dismal, protracted, nerve-racking. Nor was that all, for they could now discern the pat-pat, pat-pat of footsteps—long, soft, loping footsteps, as of huge furry paws or naked human feet. However, they could see nothing—nothing but blackness, intensified by the feeble flickering of the droshky's lanterns.

"Faster! drive faster!" Anno shouted, turning round and poking the coachman in the ribs with her umbrella. "Do you want us all to be eaten?"

"I can't mistress, I can't!" the man expostulated; "the horses are outstripping the wind as it is. They can't go quicker." And the driver, consigning Stanislaus and his sister to the innermost recesses of hell, prayed to the Virgin to save him.

Nearer and nearer drew the steps, and again a cry—a cry close behind them, perhaps fifty yards—fifty yards at the most. And as they were trying to locate it there burst into view a gigantic figure—nude and luminous, a figure that glowed like a glow-worm and bent slightly forward as it ran. It covered the ground with long, easy, swinging strides, without any apparent effort. In general form its body was like that of a man, saving that the limbs were longer and covered with short hair, and the feet and hands, besides being larger as a whole, had longer toes and fingers. Its head was partly human, partly lupine—the skull, ears, teeth, and eyes were those of a wolf, whilst the remaining features were those of a man. Its complexion was devoid of colour, startlingly white; its eyes green and lurid, its expression hellish.

Stanislaus and Anno did not know what to make of it. Was it

some terrible monstrosity that had escaped from a show, or something that was peculiar to the forest itself, something generated by the giant trees and dark, silent road? In their sublime terror they shrieked aloud, beat the air with their hands to ward it off, and finally left their seats to cling on to the back of the driver's box.

But it came nearer, nearer, and nearer, until they were almost within reach of its arms. They read death in the glinting greenness of its eyes and in the flashing of its long bared teeth. The climax of their agony, they argued, could no longer be postponed. The thing had only to make a grab at them and they would die of horror—die even before it touched them. But this was not to be.

They were still staring into the pale malevolent face drawing nearer and nearer, and wondering when the long twitching fingers would catch them by the throats, when the droshky with a mad swirl forward cleared the forest, and they found themselves gazing wildly into empty moonlit space, with no sign of their pursuer anywhere.

An hour later they narrated their adventure to the Baron. Nothing could have exceeded his distress. "My dear friends!" he said, "I owe you a profound apology. I ought to have told my man to choose any other road rather than that through the forest, which is well known to be haunted. According to rumour, a werwolf—we have good reason to believe in werwolfs here—was killed there many years ago."

CHAPTER IV

# How to Become a Werwolf

AS I HAVE already stated, in some people lycanthropy is hereditary; and when it is not hereditary it may be acquired through the performance of certain of the rites ordained by Black Magic. For the present I can only deal with the more general features of these rites (which vary according to locality) and the conditions of mind essential to those who would successfully practise these rites. In the first place, it is necessary that the person desirous of acquiring the property of lycanthropy should be in earnest and a believer in those superphysical powers whose favour he is about to ask.

Assuming we have such an individual he must, first of all, betake himself to a spot remote from the haunts of men. The powers to be petitioned are not to be found promiscuously—anywhere. They favour only such waste and solitary places as the deserts, woods, and mountain-tops.

The locality chosen, our candidate must next select a night when the moon is new and strong.[2] He must then choose a perfectly

---

2 Psychic influences are demonstrated by the position of the planets. For instance, at a new moon, cusp of Seventh House, and cojoined with Saturn in opposition to Jupiter,

level piece of ground, and on it, at midnight, he must mark, either with chalk or string—it really does not matter which—a circle of not less than seven feet in radius, and within this, and from the same centre, another circle of three feet in radius. Then, in the centre of this inner circle he must kindle a fire, and over the fire place an iron tripod containing an iron vessel of water. As soon as the water begins to boil the would-be lycanthropist must throw into it handfuls of any three of the following substances: Asafœtida, parsley, opium, hemlock, henbane, saffron, aloe, poppy-seed and solanum; repeating as he does so these words:—

"Spirits from the deep
Who never sleep,
Be kind to me.

"Spirits from the grave
Without a soul to save,
Be kind to me.

"Spirits of the trees
That grow upon the leas,
Be kind to me.

"Spirits of the air,
Foul and black, not fair,
Be kind to me.

"Water spirits hateful,
To ships and bathers fateful,
Be kind to me.

---

sinister superphysical presences are much in evidence on the earth.

"Spirits of earthbound dead
That glide with noiseless tread,
Be kind to me.

"Spirits of heat and fire,
Destructive in your ire,
Be kind to me.

"Spirits of cold and ice,
Patrons of crime and vice,
Be kind to me.

"Wolves, vampires, satyrs, ghosts!
Elect of all the devilish hosts!I pray you send hither,
Send hither, send hither,
The great grey shape that makes men shiver!
Shiver, shiver, shiver!
Come! Come! Come!"

The supplicant then takes off his vest and shirt and smears his body with the fat of some newly killed animal (preferably a cat), mixed with aniseed, camphor, and opium. Then he binds round his loins a girdle made of wolf's-skin, and kneeling down within the circumference of the first circle, waits for the advent of the Unknown. When the fire burns blue and quickly dies out, the Unknown is about to manifest itself; if it does not then actually appear it will make its presence felt.

There is little consistency in the various methods of the spirit's advent: sometimes a deep unnatural silence immediately precedes it; sometimes crashes and bangs, groanings and shriekings, herald its approach. When it remains invisible its presence is indicated and accompanied by a sensation of abnormal cold and the most acute terror. It is sometimes visible in the guise of a huntsman—which is, perhaps, its most popular shape—sometimes in the form of a monstrosity, partly man and partly beast—and sometimes it is seen ill defined and only partially materialized. To what order of spirits it belongs is, of course, purely a matter of conjecture. I believe it to be some malevolent, superphysical, creative power, such as, in my opinion, participated largely in the creation of this and other planets. I do not believe it to be the Devil, because I do not believe in the existence of only one devil, but in countless devils. It is difficult to say to what extent the Unknown is believed to be powerful by those who approach it for the purpose of acquiring the gift of lycanthropy; but I am inclined to think that the majority of these, at all events, do not ascribe to it any supreme power, but regard it merely as a local spirit—the spirit of some particular wilderness or forest.

Of course, it is quite possible that the property of werwolfery might be acquired by other than a direct personal communication with the Unknown, as, for example, by eating a wolf's brains, by drinking water out of a wolf's footprints, or by drinking out of a stream from which three or more wolves have been seen to drink; but as most of the stories I have heard of werwolfery acquired in this way are of a wild and improbable nature, I think there is little to be learned from the *modus operandi* they advocate. The following story, which I believe to be true in the main, was told me by a Dr. Broniervski, whom I met in Boulogne.

"Ten years ago," my informant began, "I was engaged in a geological expedition in Montenegro. I left Cetinge in company with my escort, Dugald Dalghetty, a Dalmatian who had served me on many former occasions; but owing to an accident I was compelled to leave him behind at a village about thirty miles east of the capital. As it was absolutely necessary for me to have a guide, I chose a Montenegrin called Kniaz. Dalghetty warned me against him. 'Kniaz has the evil eye,' he said; 'he will bring misfortune on you. Choose some one else.'

"Kniaz was certainly not particularly prepossessing. He was tall and angular, and pock-marked and sandy-haired; and his eyes had a peculiar cast—only a cast, of course, nothing more. To balance these detractions he was civil in his manners and extremely moderate in his terms. Dalghetty, faithful fellow, almost wept as he watched us depart. 'I shall never see you again,' he said. 'Never!'

"Just outside the last cottage in the village we passed a gigantic, broad-shouldered man, clad in the usual clothes of frieze, a black skullcap, wide trousers, and tights from the knee to the ankle. Over his shoulders was a new white strookah, of which he seemed very proud; whilst he had a perfect armament of weapons—rifles, pistols, yatagan—polished up to the knocker—and cartouche-box. He was conversing with a girl at one of the windows, but turned as we came up to him and leered impudently at Kniaz. The sallow in Kniaz's cheeks turned to white, and the cast in his eyes became ten times more pronounced. But he said nothing—only drooped his head and shuffled a little closer to me.

"For the rest of the day he spoke little; and I could tell from his expression and general air of dejection that he was still brooding over the incident. The following morning—we stayed the night in a wayside inn—Kniaz informed me that the route we had intended taking to Skaravoski—the town I meant to make the head quarters for my daily excursions—was blocked (a blood feud had suddenly been declared between two tribes), and that consequently we should have to go by some other way. I inquired who had told him and whether he was sure the information was correct. He replied that our host had given him the warning, and that the possibility of such an occurrence had been suggested to him before leaving Cetinge. 'But,' he added, 'there is no need to worry, for the other road, though somewhat wild and rough, is, in reality, quite as safe, and certainly a good league and a half shorter.' As it made no very great difference to me which way I went, I acquiesced. There was no reason to suspect Kniaz of any sinister motive—cases of treachery on the part of escorts are practically unknown in Montenegro—and if it were true that some of the tribes were engaged in a vendetta, then I certainly agreed that we could not give them too wide a berth. At the same time I could not help observing a strange innovation in Kniaz's character. Besides the sullenness that had laid hold of him since his encounter with the man and girl, he now exhibited a restless eagerness—his eyes were never still, his lips constantly moved, and I could frequently hear him muttering to himself as we trudged along. He asked me several times if I believed in the supernatural, and when I laughingly replied 'No, I am far too practical and level-headed,' he said 'Wait. We are now in the land of spirits. You will soon change your opinion.'

"The country we were traversing was certainly forbidding—forbidding enough to be the hunting ground of legions of ferocious animals. But the supernatural! Bah! I flouted such an idea. All day we journeyed along a lofty ridge, from which, shortly before dusk, it became necessary to descend by a narrow and precipitous declivity, full of danger and difficulty. At the bottom we halted three or four hours, to wait for the moon, in a position sufficiently romantic and uncomfortable. A north-east wind, cold and biting, came whistling over the hills, and seemed to be sucked down into the hollow where we sat on the chilly stones. The moment we sighted the slightly depressed orb of the moon over the vast hill of rocks, and the Milky Way spanning the heavens with a brilliancy seen only in the East, we pushed on again. On, along a painfully rough and uneven track, flanked on either side by perpendicular masses of rock that reared themselves, black and frowning, like some huge ruined wall. On, till we eventually came to the end of the defile. Then an extraordinary scene burst upon us.

"Whilst the irregular line of rocks continued close on our left, beyond it—glittering in the miraculously magnifying moonlight with more gigantic proportions than nature had afforded—was a huge pile of white rocks, looking like the fortifications of some vast fabulous city. There were yawning gateways flanked by bastions of great altitude; towers and pyramids; crescents and domes; and dizzy pinnacles; and castellated heights; all invested with the unearthly grandeur of the moon, yet showing in their wide breaches and indescribable ruin sure proofs that during a long course of ages they had been battered and undermined by rain, hurricane, and lightning, and all the mighty artillery of time. Piled on one another, and repeated over and over again, these strangely contorted rocks stretched as far as the eye could reach, sinking, however, as they receded, and leading the mind, though not the eye, down to the plain below, through which a turbid stream wound its way rebelliously, like some great twisting, twirling, silvery-scaled serpent.

"It was into this gorge that Kniaz in a voice thrilling with excitement informed me we must plunge.

"'It is called,' he explained to me, 'the haunted valley, and it is said to have been from time immemorial under the spell of the grey spirits—a species of phantasm, half man and half animal, that have the power of metamorphosing men into wild beasts.' Horses, he went on to inform me, showed the greatest reluctance to enter the valley, which was a sure proof that the place was in very truth phantom-ridden. I must say its appearance favoured that theory. The path by which we descended was almost perpendicular, and filled with shadows. Precipices hemmed us in on every side; and here and there a huge fragment of rock, standing like a petrified giant, its summit gleaming white in the moonbeams, barred our way.

"On reaching the bottom we found ourselves exactly opposite the pile of white rocks, at the base of which roared the stream. Kniaz now declared that our best plan was to halt and bivouac here for the night. I expostulated, saying that I did not feel in the least degree tired, that the spot was far from comfortable, and that I preferred to push on. Kniaz then pleaded that he was too exhausted to proceed, and, in fact, whined to such an extent that in the end I gave way, and lying down under cover of a boulder, tried to imagine myself in bed. I did actually fall asleep, and awoke with the sensation of something crawling over my face. Sitting up, I looked around for Kniaz—he was nowhere to be seen. The oddness of his behaviour, his alternate talkativeness and sullenness, and the anxiety he had manifested to come by this route, made me at last suspicious. Had he any ulterior motive in leading me hither? What had become of him?

Where was he? I got up and approached the margin of the stream, and then for the first time I felt frightened. The illimitable possibilities of that enormous mass of castellated rocks towering above me both quelled and fascinated me. Were these flickering shadows shadows, or—or had Kniaz, after all, spoken the truth when he said this valley was haunted? The moonlight rendered every object I looked upon so startlingly vivid, that not even the most trivial detail escaped my notice, and the more I scrutinized the more firmly the conviction grew on me that I was in a neighbourhood differing essentially from any spot I had hitherto visited. I saw nothing with which I had been formerly conversant. The few trees at hand resembled no growth of either the torrid, temperate, or northern frigid zones, and were altogether unlike those of the southern latitudes with which I was most familiar. The very rocks were novel in their mass, their colour, and their stratification; and the stream itself, utterly incredible as it may appear, had so little in common with the streams of other countries that I shrank away from it in alarm. I am at a loss to give any distinct idea of the nature of the water. I can only say it was not like ordinary water, either in appearance or behaviour. Even in the moonlight it was not colourless, nor was it of any one colour, presenting to the eye every variety of green and blue. Although it fell over stones and rocks with the same rapid descent as ordinary water, it made no sound, neither splash nor gurgle. Summoning up courage, I dipped my fingers in the stream; it was quite cold and limpid. The difference did not lie there. I was still puzzling over this phenomenon, still debating in my mind the possibility of the valley being haunted, when I heard a cry—a peculiarly ominous cry—human and yet animal. For a few seconds I was too overcome with fear to move. At last, however, having in some measure pulled myself together, I ventured cautiously in the direction of the noise, and after treading as lightly as I could over the rough and rocky soil for some couple of hundred yards, suddenly came to an abrupt standstill.

"Kneeling beside the stream with its back turned to me was an extraordinary figure—a thing with a man's body and an animal's head—a dark, shaggy head with unmistakable prick ears. I gazed at it aghast. What was it? What was it doing? As I stared it bent down, lapped the water, and raising its head, uttered the same harrowing sound that had brought me thither. I then saw, with a fresh start of wonder, that its hands, which shone very white in the moonlight, were undergoing a gradual metamorphosis. I watched carefully, and first one finger, and then another, became amalgamated in a long, furry paw, armed with sharp, formidable talons.

"I suppose that in my fear and astonishment I made some sound of sufficient magnitude to attract attention; anyhow, the creature at once swung round, and, with a snarl of rage, rushed savagely at me. Being unarmed, and also, I confess, unnerved, I completely lost my presence of mind, and not attempting to escape—though flight would have been futile, for I was nothing of a runner—shrieked aloud for help. The thing sprang at me, its jaws wide open, its eyes red with rage. I struck at it wildly, and have dim recollections of my puny blows landing on its face. It closed in on me, and gripping me tightly round the body with its sinewy arms, hurled me to the ground. My head came in violent contact with a stone, and I lost consciousness. On recovering my senses, I was immeasurably surprised to find Dalghetty sitting on a rock watching me, whilst close beside him was Kniaz, bloodstained and motionless.

"Dalghetty explained the situation. 'Convinced that evil would befall you in the company of such a man,' he said, pointing to the figure at his feet, 'I determined to set out in pursuit of you. By a miracle, which I attribute to Our Lady, the effects of my accident suddenly wore off, and I felt absolutely well. I borrowed a horse, and, starting from Cetinge at nine this morning, reached the inn where you passed last night at eleven. There I learned the route you had taken, and leaving the horse behind—on such a road I was safer on my legs—I pressed on. The ground, being moist in places, revealed your footprints, and I had no difficulty at all in tracing you to the bottom of the declivity. There I was at sea for some moments, since the rocky soil was too hard to receive any impressions. But hearing the howl of some wild animal, I concluded you were attacked, and, guided by the sound, I arrived here to find a werwolf actually preparing to devour you. A bullet from my rifle speedily rendered the creature harmless, and a close inspection of it proved that my surmises were only too correct. It was none other than our friend here with the evil eye—Kniaz!'

"'Kniaz a werwolf!' I ejaculated.

"'Yes! he inveigled you here because he had made up his mind to drink the water of the enchanted stream, and so become metamorphosed from a man to a wild beast. His object in doing so was to destroy a young farmer who had stolen his sweetheart, and for whom he, as a man, was no match. However, he is harmless now, but it is a warning to you in future to trust no one who has the evil eye.'"

Belief in the evil eye is everywhere prevalent in the East, and it is undoubtedly true that people who have certain peculiarities in their eyes, both with regard to expression, colour, and formation, are people to be avoided. If malevolently inclined, they invariably bring ill-luck on all who become acquainted with them. I have followed the careers of several people in whom I have noticed this baneful feature, and their histories have been one long tale of sin or sorrow—often both.

But though the evil eye denotes an evil superphysical influence, the werwolf is not necessarily possessed of it. Sometimes a werwolf may be told by the long, straight, slanting eyebrows, which meet in an angle over the nose; sometimes by the hands, the third finger of which is a trifle the longest; or by the finger-nails, which are red, almond-shaped, and curved; sometimes by the ears, which are set rather low, and far back on their heads; and sometimes by a noticeably long, swinging stride, which is strongly suggestive of some animal. Either one or other of these features is always present in hereditary werwolves, and is also frequently developed in those people who become werwolves, either at the same time as or soon after they acquire the property.

CHAPTER V

# Werwolves and Exorcism

**IN THE PRECEDING** chapter I touched on one or two modes of evoking the spirits that have it in their power to confer the property of lycanthropy; I now pass on to the question of exorcism in relation to werwolves.

Is it possible to exorcize the evil power of metamorphosis possessed by the werwolf, or, as those would say who see in the werwolf, not the possession of a property, but a spirit, "to exorcize the evil spirit"?

For my own part, and basing my opinion on my own experiences with other forms of the superphysical, with regard to the success of exorcism I am sceptical. I have been present when exorcism has been tried—tried on people supposed to be obsessed with demoniacal spirits, and tried on spontaneous psychic phenomena in haunted houses—and in both cases it has failed. Now, although, as I have said, I regard lycanthropy in the light of a property, and do not believe in the lycanthropist being possessed of a separate individual spirit, I am inclined to think, were exorcism efficacious at all, that it would take effect on werwolves, since the property of werwolfery is a gift which is, more or less, directly acquired from the malevolent spirits.

But I am not only dubious as to the powers of exorcism generally, I am also dubious as to its effect on werwolves. I have come across a good many alleged cases of its having been successfully practised on werwolves, but in regard to these cases, the authority is not very reliable, nor the corroborative evidence strong.

Nearly all the methods prescribed embrace the use of some potion; such, for example, as sulphur, asafœtida, and castoreum, mixed with clear spring water; or hypericum, compounded with vinegar—which two potions seem to have been (and to be still) the most favoured recipes for removing the devilish power.

The ceremony of exorcism proceeded as follows: The werwolf was sprinkled three times with one of the above solutions, and saluted with the sign of the cross, or addressed thrice by his baptismal name, each address being accompanied by a blow on the forehead with a knife; or he was sprinkled, whilst at the same time his girdle was removed; or in lieu of being sprinkled, he had three drops of blood drawn from his chest, or was compelled to kneel in one spot for a great number of years.

A full description of the practice and failure of exorcism was cited to me the other day in connexion with a comparatively recent happening in Asiatic Russia:—

Tina Peroviskei, a wealthy young widow, who lived in St. Nicholas Street, Moscow—not a hundred yards from the house of Herr Schauman, the well-known German banker and horticulturist (every one in Russia has heard of the Schauman tulips)—met a gentleman named Ivan Baranoff at a friend's house, and, despite the warning of her brother, married him.

Ivan Baranoff did not look more than thirty years of age. He was usually dressed in grey furs—a grey fur coat, grey fur leggings, and a grey fur cap. His features were very handsome—at least, so Tina thought—his hair was flaxen, glossy, and bright as a mirror; and his mouth, when open, displayed a most brilliant set of even, white teeth. Tina had three children by her first husband, and the fuss Ivan Baranoff made of them pleased her immensely. Their own father never evinced a greater anxiety for their welfare. Ivan brought them the most expensive toys and sweetmeats—particularly sweetmeats—and would insist on seeing for himself that they had plenty of rich, creamy milk, fresh eggs, and the best of butter.

"You'll kill them with kindness," Tina often remonstrated. "They are too fat by half now."

"They can't be too fat," Ivan would reply. "No one is too fat. I love to see rosy cheeks and stout limbs. Wait till you're in the country! Then you may talk about putting on flesh. The air there will fatten you even more than the food."

"Then we shall burst, and there will be an end of us," Tina would laughingly say.

But despite all this, despite the way in which he fondled and caressed them, the children involuntarily shrank away from Ivan; and on Tina angrily demanding the reason, they told her they could not help it—there was something in his bright eyes and touch that frightened them. When Tina's brothers and sisters heard of this, they upheld the children.

"We are not in the least surprised," they said; "his eyes are cruel—so are his lips; and as for his eyebrows—those dark, straight eyebrows that meet in a point over the nose—why, every one knows what a bad sign that is!"

But Tina grew so angry they had to desist. "You are jealous," she said to her brothers. "You envy him his looks and money." And to her sisters she said, "You only wish you could have had him yourselves. You know I love him already far more than I ever loved Rupert." (Rupert was her first husband.)

And within a month or so of the marriage Tina left all her relatives in Moscow, and, accompanied by her children and dogs—some people hinted that Tina was fonder of her dogs than of her children—went with Ivan Baranoff to his ancestral home near Orsk.

Though accustomed to the cold, Tina found the climate of Orsk almost more than she could bear. Her husband's house, which occupied an extremely solitary position on the confines of a gloomy forest, some few miles from the town, was a large, grey stone building full of dark winding passages and dungeon-like rooms. The furniture was scant, and the rooms, with the exception of those devoted to herself, her husband and the children, which were covered with crimson drugget, were carpetless. A more barren, inhospitable looking house could not be imagined, and the moment Tina entered it, her spirits sank to zero. The atmosphere of the place frightened her the most. It was not that it was merely forlorn and cheerless, but there was a something in it that reminded her of the smell of the animal houses in the Zoological Gardens in Moscow, and a something she could not analyse—a something which she concluded must be peculiar to the house. The children were very much upset. The sight of the dark entrance hall and wide, silent staircases, bathed in gloom, terrified them.

"Oh, mother!" they cried, clutching hold of Tina Baranoff and dragging her back, "we can never live here. Take us away at once. Look at those things. Whatever are they?" And they pointed to the shadows—queerly shaped shadows—that lay in thick clusters on the stairs and all around them.

Tina did not know what to say. Her own apprehensions and the only too obvious terror of the dogs, whom she had literally to drive across the threshold, and who whined and cringed at her feet, confirming the children's fears, made it impossible for her to check them. Moreover, since leaving Moscow the warnings of her friends and relations had often come back to her. Though Ivan had never ceased to be kind, his conduct roused her suspicions. During the journey, which he had insisted should be performed in a droshky, he halted every evening directly the moon became invisible, and used to disappear regularly between dusk and sunrise. He would never tell her where he went or attempt to explain the oddness of his conduct, but when pressed by her would merely say:

"It is a habit. I always like to roam abroad in the night-time—it would be very bad for my health if I did not."

And this was all Tina could get out of him. She noticed, too, what her blind infatuation had prevented her observing before, that there was a fierce expression in his eyes when he set out on these nocturnal rambles, and that on his return the corners of his mouth and his long finger-nails were always smeared with blood. Furthermore, she noticed that although he was concerned about the appetites of herself and the children, he ate very little cooked food himself—never vegetables or bread—and would often furtively put a raw piece of meat into his mouth when he thought no one was looking.

Tina hoped that these irregularities would cease on their arrival at the château, but, on the contrary, they rather increased, and she became greatly perturbed.

The second night after their arrival, when she had been in bed some time and was nearly asleep, Tina, between her half-closed eyelids, watched her husband get out of bed, stealthily open the window, and drop from the sill. Some hours later she was again aroused. She heard the growl of a wolf—and immediately afterwards saw Ivan's grey-clad head at the window. He came softly into the room, and as he tiptoed across the floor to the washstand, Tina saw splashes of blood on his face and coat, whilst it dripped freely from his finger-tips. In the morning the news was brought her by the children that one of her favourite dogs was dead—eaten by some wild animal, presumably a wolf. Tina's position now became painful in the extreme. She was more than suspicious of her husband, and had no one—saving her children—in whom she could confide. The house seemed to be under a ban; no one, not even a postman or tradesman, ever came near it, and with the exception of the two servants, whose silent, gliding movements and light glittering eyes filled both her and her children with infinite dread, she did not see a soul.

On four consecutive nights one of her four dogs was killed, each in precisely the same manner; and on each of these consecutive nights Tina watched Ivan surreptitiously leave the house and return all bloodstained, and accompanied by the distant howl of wolves. And on the day following the death of each dog respectively, Tina noticed the grey glinting eyes of the two servants become more and more earnestly fixed on the children and herself. At meal-times the eyes never left her; she was conscious of their scrutiny at every mouthful she took; and when she passed them in the passages, she instinctively felt their gaze following her steadily till she was out of sight. Sometimes, hearing a stealthy breathing outside her room, she would quickly open the door, demanding who was there; and she invariably caught one or other of the servants slinking away disconcerted, but still peeping at her furtively from under his long pointed eyebrows. When she spoke to them they answered her in harsh, curiously discordant tones, and usually only in monosyllables; but she never heard them converse with one another save in whispers—always in whispers. The house was now full of shadows—and whispers. They haunted her even in her sleep. For the first two or three days her husband had been communicative; but he gradually grew more and more taciturn, until at last he rarely said anything at all. He merely watched her—watched her wherever she went, and whatever she did; and he watched the children—particularly the children—with the same expression, the same undefinable secretive expression that harmonized so well with the shadows and whispers. And it was this treatment—the treatment she now received from her husband—that made Tina appreciate the company of her children. Before, they had been quite a tertiary consideration—Ivan had come first; then the dogs; and lastly, Hilda, Olga, and Peter. But this order was at length reversed; and on the death of the last of her pets, Hilda, Olga and Peter stood first. She spent practically every minute of the day with them; and, despite the protestations of her husband, converted her dressing-room into a bedroom for them. The first evening of their removal to their new quarters, Tina sat and played with them till one after another they fell asleep from sheer exhaustion. Then she sat beside them and examined them curiously. Hilda, the eldest, was lying composed and orderly, with pale cheek and smooth hair, her limbs straight, her head slightly bent, the bedclothes unruffled upon the regularly heaving chest. How pretty Hilda looked, and how odd it was that she, Tina, had never noticed the beauty of the child before! Why, with her fair complexion, delicate features, and perfectly shaped arms and hands she would undoubtedly one day take all Moscow by storm; and every one would say, "Do you know who that lovely girl is? She is the daughter of Tina—Tina Baranoff. [She shuddered at the name Baranoff.] No wonder she is beautiful!"

Tina turned from Hilda to Olga. What a contrast, but not an unpleasant one—for Olga was pretty, too, though in a different style. What a sight!—defying all order and bursting all bounds, flushed, tumbled and awry—the round arms tossed up, the rosy face flung back, the bedclothes pushed off, the pillow flung out, the nightcap one way, the hair another—all that was disorderly and lovely by night, all that was unruly and winning by day. Tina—dainty, elegant, perfumed, manicured Tina—bent over untidy little Olga and kissed her.

Then she turned to Peter, and, unable to resist the temptation, tickled his toes and woke him. When she had at last sent him to sleep again, it was almost dinner-time; and she had barely got into her dress when one of the servants rapped at the door to say that the meal was ready. The house was very large, and Tina had to pass through two halls and down a long corridor before reaching the room where the dinner was served. Rather to her relief than otherwise, her husband did not put in an appearance, and a note from him informed her that he had unexpectedly been called away on business and would not be able to return till late the following day.

Tina did not enjoy her dinner. The soup had rather a peculiar flavour, but she knew it was useless to make any comment. The servants either could not or would not understand, and Ivan invariably upheld them in everything they did. Unable to bear the man's eyes continually fixed on her, she told him not to wait, and hurried through the meal so as to get him out of the way, and be left for the rest of the evening in peace. The big wood fire appealed to Tina—it was the only thing in that part of the house that seemed to have any life—and she resolved to sit by it, and, perhaps, skim through a book. Tina seldom read—in Moscow, all her evenings were spent at cards. She remembered, however, that somebody had told her repeatedly, and emphatically, that she ought to read Tolstoy's "Resurrection," and she had actually brought it with her. Now she would wade through it. But whether it was the heat of the fire, or the lateness of the hour, or both, her senses grew more and more drowsy, and before she had begun to read, she fell asleep.

She was, at length, partially awakened by a loud noise. At first her sleepy senses paid little attention and she dozed on. But again she was roused. A noise which grew louder and louder at last compelled her to shake off sleep, and starting up, she opened the door and looked into the passage. A few streaks of moonlight, streaming through an iron grating high up in the wall, enabled her to see a tall figure stealing softly along the corridor, with its back towards her. The thing was so extraordinary that for a moment or so she fancied she must still be dreaming; but the cold night air blowing freely in her face speedily assured her that what she saw was grim reality. The thing was a monstrosity, a hideous hybrid of man and beast, and as she gazed at it, too horror-stricken to move, a second and third form exactly similar to it crept out from among the shadows against the wall and joined it. And Tina, yielding to a sudden fascination, followed in their wake. In this fashion they crossed the hall and ascended the staircase, Tina keeping well behind them. She knew where they were aiming for, and any little doubt that she might have had was set at rest, when they turned into the passage leading to her bedroom. A moaning cry of fear from one of the children told her that they, too, knew by intuition of their coming danger. Tina was now in an agony of mind as to what to do for the best. That the intention of these hideous creatures—be they what they might—phantasms or things of flesh and blood—was sinister, she had not the slightest doubt; but how could she prevent them getting at her children? The most she could do would be to shout to Hilda and tell her to lock the two doors. But would that keep them out? She opened her mouth and jerked out "Hilda!" She tried again, but her throat had completely dried up, and she could not articulate another syllable. The sound, however, though faint, had been sufficient to attract the attention of the hindermost creature. It turned, and the light from the moon, coming through the half-open door of her bedroom, shone on its glittering eyes and white teeth. It sprang towards her. With one convulsive bound Tina cleared the threshold of a room immediately behind her, dashed the door to—locked it—barred it—flung a chair against it; and stood in an agony, for which no words exist. She seemed to see, all in a moment, herself safe, and her children—not a door closed between them and those dreadful jaws! She then became stupefied with terror, and a strange, dinning sound, like the pulsation of her heart, filled her ears and shut out every sense.

"It is a devil! a devil!" she repeated mechanically; and then, forcing herself out of the trance-like feeling that oppressed her, she combated with the cowardice that prevented her rushing out—if only to die in an attempt to save her children. She had not realized till then that it was possible to care for them more even—much more even—than she had cared for her dogs. She placed one hand on the lock, and looked round for some weapon of defence. There was not a thing she could use—not a stanchion to the window, not a rod to the bed. And even if there had been, how futile in her puny grip! She glanced at her tiny white fingers with their carefully trimmed and polished nails, and smiled—a grim smile of irony. Then she placed her ear against the panels of the door and listened—and from the other side came the sound of heavy panting and the stealthy movement of hands. Suddenly a scream rang out, so clear and vibrating, so full of terror, that her heart stood still and her blood congealed. It was Hilda! Hilda shrieking "Mother!" There it was again, "Mother! Mother! Help! Help!" Then a series of savage snarls and growls and more shrieks—the combined shrieks of all three children. Shrieks and growls were then mingled together in one dreadful, hideous pandemonium, which all of a sudden ceased, and was succeeded by the loud crunching and cracking of bones. At last that, too, ceased, and Tina heard footsteps rapidly approaching her door. For a moment the room and everything in it swam round her. She felt choked; the dinning in her ears came again, it beat louder and louder and completely paralysed her. A crash on the door panel, however, abruptly restored her faculties, and the idea of escaping by the window for the first time entered her mind. If her husband could use the window as a means of exit, why couldn't she? Not a second was to be lost—the creatures outside were now striving their utmost to get in. It was the work of a moment to throw open the window, and almost before she knew she had opened it, she found herself standing on the ground beneath. The night had grown darker; she could not see the path; she knew that she was losing time, and yet that all depended on her haste; she felt fevered with impatience, yet torpid with terror. At length she disengaged herself from the broken, uneven soil on to which she had dropped, and struggled forward. On and on she went, not knowing where her next step would land her, and dreading every moment to hear the steps of her pursuers. The darkness of the night favoured her, and by dodging in and out the bushes and never keeping to the same track, although still keeping a forward course, she successfully eluded her enemies, whose hoarse cries gradually grew fainter and fainter. By good luck she reached the high road, which eventually brought her to Orsk; and there she sought shelter in a hotel. In the morning, on learning from the landlord that a friend of hers, a Colonel Majendie, was in the town, Tina sought him out, and into his sympathizing ears poured the story of her adventures.

Now it so happened that a priest of the name of Rappaport, a friend of the Colonel's, came in before Tina had finished her story, and on being told what had happened, declared that Ivan Baranoff and his servants had long been suspected of being werwolves. He then begged that before anything was done to them he might be allowed to try his powers of exorcism. The Colonel ridiculed the idea, but in the end was persuaded to postpone his visit to the château till the evening, and to go there with an escort, a quartette of his most trusted soldiers, and accompanied by his friend the Rev. Father Rappaport. Accordingly, at about nine o'clock the party set out, and, on arriving at the house, found it in total darkness and apparently deserted.

But they had not waited long before a series of savage growls from the adjacent thicket put them on their guard, and almost immediately afterwards three werwolves stalked across the path and prepared to enter the house. At a word from the Colonel the soldiers leaped forward, and after a most desperate scuffle, in which they were all more or less badly mauled, succeeded in securing their quarry. In more civilized parts of the country the police would have been called in, but here, where that good old law, "Might is right," still held good, a man in the Colonel's position could do whatever he deemed most expedient, and Colonel Majendie had made up his mind that justice should no longer be delayed. The château had borne an ill reputation for generations. From time immemorial Ivan Baranoff's ancestors had been suspected of lycanthropy, and this last deed of the family was their crowning atrocity.

"You may exorcize the devils first," the Colonel grimly remarked to the priest, wiping the blood off his sleeves. "We will hang and quarter the brutes afterwards."

To this the holy Father willingly agreed, for he did not care what happened so long as his exorcism was successful.

The rites that were performed in connexion with this ceremony (and which I understand are those most commonly observed in exorcizing all manner of evil spirits) were as follows:—

A circle of seven feet radius was drawn on the ground in white chalk. At the centre of the circle were inscribed, in yellow chalk, certain magical figures representing Mercury, and about them was drawn, in white chalk, a triangle within a circle of three feet radius—the centre of the circle being the same as that of the outer circle. Within this inner circle were then placed the three captive werwolves. It would be well to explain here that in exorcism, as well as in the evocation of spirits, great attention must be paid to the position of the stars, as astrology exercises the greatest influence on the spirit world. The present occasion, the reverend Father pointed out, was specially favourable for the casting out of devils, since from 8.32 p.m. to 9.16 p.m. was under the dominion of the great angel Mercury—the most bitter opponent of all evil spirits; that is to say, Mercury was in 17° ♊. on the cusp of Seventh House, slightly to south of due west.

☽ going to ♂ with ☿ in 14° ♊.

☿ to ♂ ♆ ☿ 130° ♄

Round the outer circle the reverend Father now proceeded to place, at equal intervals, hand-lamps, burning olive oil. He then erected a rude altar of wood, about a foot to the southeast of the circumference of the inner circle. Exactly opposite this altar, and about

1-1/2 feet to the far side of the circumference of the inner circle, he ordered the soldiers to build a fire, and to place over it a tripod and pot, the latter containing two pints of pure spring water.

He then prepared a mixture consisting of these ingredients:—

2 drachms of sulphur.

1/2 oz. of castoreum.

6 drachms of opium.

3 drachms of asafœtida.

1/2 oz. of hypericum.

3/4 oz. of ammonia.

1/2 oz. of camphor.

When this was thoroughly mixed he put it in the water in the pot, adding to it a portion of a mandrake root, a live snake, two live toads in linen bags, and a fungus. He then bound together, with red tape, a wand consisting of three sprigs taken, respectively, from an ash, birch, and white poplar.

He next proceeded to pray, kneeling in front of the altar; and continued praying till the unearthly cries of the toads announced the fact that the water, in which they were immersed, was beginning to boil. Slowly getting up and crossing himself, he went to the fire, and dipping a cup in the pot, solemnly approached the werwolves, and slashing them severely across the head with his wand, dashed in their faces the seething liquid, calling out as he did so: "In the name of Our Blessed Lady I command thee to depart. Black, evil devils from hell, begone! Begone! Again I say, Begone!" He repeated this three times to the vociferous yells of the smarting werwolves, who struggled so frantically that they succeeded in bursting their bonds, and, leaping to their feet, endeavoured to escape into the bushes. The soldiers at once rose in pursuit and the priest was left alone. He had got rid of the flesh and blood, and he presumed he had got rid of the devils. But that remained to be proved.

In the chase that ensued one of the werwolves was shot, and, simultaneously with death, metamorphosis into the complete form of a huge grey wolf took place. The other two eluded their pursuers for some time, but were eventually tracked owing to the discovery of the half-eaten remains of an old woman and two children in a cave. True to their lupine natures,[3] they showed no fight when cornered, and a couple of well-directed bullets put an end to their existence—the same metamorphosis occurring in their case as in the case of their companion. With the death of the three werwolves the château, one would naturally have thought, might have emerged from its ban. But no such thing. It speedily acquired a reputation for being haunted.

And that it was haunted—haunted not only by werwolves but by all sorts of ghastly phantasms—I have no doubt.

I was told, not long ago, that Tina, whose property it became, pulled it down, and that another house, replete with every modern luxury—but equally haunted [4] now marks the site of the old château.

---

3 The wolf and puma, alone among savage animals, give in directly they are brought to bay.

4 The hauntings in houses are often due to something connected with the ground on which the houses are built.

## CHAPTER VI

# The Werwolf in the British Isles

IT IS COMMONLY known that there were once wolves in Great Britain and Scotland. Whilst history tells us of a king who tried to get rid of them by offering so much for every wolf's head that was brought to him, we read in romance how Llewellyn slew Gelert, the faithful hound that, having slain the wolf, saved his infant's life; and tradition has handed down to us many other stories of them. But the news that werwolves, too, once flourished in these climes will come as a surprise to many.

Yet Halliwell, quoting from a Bodleian MS., says: "Ther ben somme that eten chyldren and men, and eteth noon other flesh fro that tyme that thei be a-charmed with mannys flesh for rather thei wolde be deed; and thei be cleped werewolfes for men shulde be war of them."

Nor is this the only reference to them in ancient chronicles, for Gervase of Tilbury, in his "Otia Imperiala," writes:—

"Vidimus enim frequenter in Anglia per lunationes homines in lupos mutari, quod hominum genus gerulphos Galli nominant, Angli vero were-wulf dicunt." And Richard Verstegan, in his "Restitution of Decayed Intelligence," 1605, says: "The were-wolves are certain sorcerers who having anointed their bodies with an ointment which they make by the instinct of the devil, and putting on a certain enchanted girdle, do not only unto the view of others seem as wolves, but to their own thinking have both the shape and nature of wolves, so long as they wear the said girdle; and they do dispose themselves as very wolves in worrying and killing, and eating most of human creatures."

In my investigations of haunted houses and my psychical research work generally, I have come across much that I believe to be good evidence in support of the testimony of these writers. For instance, in localities once known to have been the favourite haunts of wolves, I have met people who have informed me they have seen phantasms, in shape half human and half beast, that might well be the earth-bound spirits of werwolves.

A Miss St. Denis told me she was once staying on a farm, in Merionethshire, where she witnessed a phenomenon of this class. The farm, though some distance from the village, was not far off the railway station, a very diminutive affair, with only one platform and a mere box that served as a waiting-room and booking-office combined. It was, moreover, one of those stations where the separate duties of station-master, porter, booking-clerk, and ticket-collector are performed by one and the same person, and where the signal always appears to be down. As the platform commanded the only paintable view in the neighbourhood, Miss St. Denis often used to resort there with her sketch-book. On one occasion she had stayed rather later than usual, and on rising hurriedly from her camp-stool saw, to her surprise, a figure which she took to be that of a man, sitting on a truck a few yards distant, peering at her. I say to her surprise, because, excepting on the rare occasion of a train arriving, she had never seen anyone at the station besides the station-master, and in the evening the platform was invariably deserted. The loneliness of the place was for the first time brought forcibly home to her. The station-master's tiny house was at least some hundred yards away, and beyond that there was not another habitation nearer than the farm. On all sides of her, too, were black, frowning precipices, full of seams and fissures and inequalities, showing vague and shadowy in the fading rays of the sun. Here and there were the huge, gaping mouths of gloomy slate quarries that had long been disused, and were now half full of foul water. Around them the earth was heaped with loose fragments of rock which had evidently been detached from the principal mass and shivered to pieces in the fall. A few trees, among which were the black walnut, the slippery elm, and here and there an oak, grew among the rocks, and attested by their dwarfish stature the ungrateful soil in which they had taken root. It was not an exhilarating scene, but it was one that had a peculiar fascination for Miss St. Denis—a fascination she could not explain, and which she now began to regret. The darkness had come on very rapidly, and was especially concentrated, so it seemed to her, round the spot where she sat, and she could make nothing out of the silent figure on the truck, save that it had unpleasantly bright eyes and there was something queer about it. She coughed to see if that would have any effect, and as it had none she coughed again. Then she spoke and said, "Can you tell me the time, please?" But there was no reply, and the figure still sat there staring at her. Then she grew uneasy and, packing up her things, walked out of the station, trying her best to look as if nothing had occurred. She glanced over her shoulder; the figure was following her. Quickening her pace, she assumed a jaunty air and whistled, and turning round again, saw the strange figure still coming after her. The road would soon be at its worst stage of loneliness, and, owing to the cliffs on either side of it, almost pitch dark. Indeed, the spot positively invited murder, and she might shriek herself hoarse without the remotest chance of making herself heard. To go on with this *outré* figure so unmistakably and persistently stalking her, was out of the question. Screwing up courage, she swung round, and, raising herself to her full height, cried: "What do you want? How dare you?"—She got no further, for a sudden spurt of dying sunlight, playing over the figure, showed her it was nothing human, nothing she had ever conceived possible. It was a nude grey thing, not unlike a man in body, but with a wolf's head. As it sprang forward, its light eyes ablaze with ferocity, she instinctively felt in her pocket, whipped out a pocket flash-light, and pressed the button. The effect was magical; the creature shrank back, and putting two paw-like hands in front of its face to protect its eyes, faded into nothingness.

She subsequently made inquiries, but could learn nothing beyond the fact that, in one of the quarries close to the place where the phantasm had vanished, some curious bones, partly human and partly animal, had been unearthed, and that the locality was always shunned after dusk. Miss St. Denis thought as I did, that what she had seen might very well have been the earth-bound spirit of a werwolf.

The case of another haunting of this nature was related to me last year. A young married couple of the name of Anderson, having acquired, through the death of a relative, a snug fortune, resolved to retire from business and spend the rest of their lives in indolence and ease. Being fond of the country, they bought some land in Cumberland, at the foot of some hills, far away from any town, and built on it a large two-storied villa.

They soon, however, began to experience trouble with their servants, who left them on the pretext that the place was lonely, and that they could not put up with the noises that they heard at night. The Andersons ridiculed their servants, but when their children remarked on the same thing they viewed the matter more seriously. "What are the noises like?" they inquired. "Wild animals," Willie, the eldest child, replied. "They come howling round the window at night and we hear their feet patter along the passage and stop at our door." Much mystified, Mr. and Mrs. Anderson decided to sit up with the children and listen. They did so, and between two and three in the morning were much startled by a noise that sounded like the growling of a wolf—Mr. Anderson had heard wolves in Canada—immediately beneath the window. Throwing open the window, he peered out; the moon was fully up and every stick and stone was plainly discernible; but there was now no sound and no sign of any animal. When he had closed the window the growling at once recommenced, yet when he looked again nothing was to be seen. After a while the growling ceased, and they heard the front door, which they had locked before coming upstairs, open, and the footsteps of some big, soft-footed animal ascend the stairs. Mr. Anderson waited till the steps were just outside the room and then flung open the door, but the light from his acetylene lamp revealed a passage full of moonbeams—nothing else.

He and his wife were now thoroughly mystified. In the morning they explored the grounds, but could find no trace of footmarks, nothing to indicate the nature of their visitant. It was now close on Christmas, and as the noises had not been heard for some time, it was hoped that the disturbances would not occur again. The Andersons, like all modern parents, made idols of their children. They never did wrong, nothing was too good for them, and everything they wanted they had. At Christmas, perhaps, their authority was more particularly in evidence; at any rate, it was then that the greatest care was taken that the menu should be in strict accordance with their instructions. "What shall Santa Claus bring you this time, my darlings?" Mr. Anderson asked, a week or so before the great day arrived; and Willie, aged six, at once cried out: "What a fool you are, daddy! It is all tosh about old Claus, there's no such person!"

"Wait and see!" Mr. Anderson meekly replied. "You mark my words, he will come into your room on Christmas Eve laden with presents."

"I don't believe it!" Willie retorted. "You told us that silly tale last year and I never saw any Claus!"

"He came when you were asleep, dearie," Mrs. Anderson ventured to remark.

"Well! I'll keep awake this time!" Willie shouted.

"And we'll take the presents first and pinch old Claus afterwards," Violet Evelyn, the second child, joined in.

"And I'll prick his towsers wif pins!" Horace, aged three and a half, echoed. "I don't care nothink for old Santa Claus!" and he pulled a long nose in the manner his doting father had taught him.

Christmas Eve came at last—a typical old-fashioned Christmas with heaps of snow on the ground and frost on the window-panes and trees. The Andersons' house was warm and comfortable—for once in a way the windows were shut—and enormous fires blazed merrily away in the grates. Whilst the children spent most of the day viewing the good things in the larder and speculating how much they could eat of each, and which would taste the nicest, Mr. Anderson rehearsed in full costume the rôle of Santa Claus. He had an enormous sack full of presents—everything the children had demanded—and he meant to enter their room with it on his shoulder at about twelve o'clock.

Tea-time came, and during the interval between that meal and supper all hands—even Horace's—were at work, decorating the hall and staircases with holly and mistletoe. After supper "Good King Wencelas," "Noël," and one or two other carols were sung, and the children then decided to go to bed.

It was then ten o'clock; and exactly two hours later their father, elaborately clad as Santa Claus, and staggering, in the orthodox fashion, beneath a load of presents, shuffled softly down the passage leading to their room. The snow had ceased falling, the moon was out, and the passage flooded with a soft, phosphorescent glow that threw into strong relief every minute object. Mr. Anderson had got half-way along it when on his ears there suddenly fell a faint sound of yelping! His whole frame thrilled and his mind reverted to the scenes of his youth—to the prairies in the far-off West, where, over and over again, he had heard these sounds, and his faithful Winchester repeater had stood him in good service. Again the yelping—this time nearer. Yes! it was undoubtedly a wolf; and yet there was an intonation in that yelping not altogether wolfish—something Mr. Anderson had never heard before, and which he was consequently at a loss to define. Again it rang out—much nearer this time—much more trying to the nerves, and the cold sweat of fear burst out all over him. Again—close under the wall of the house—a moaning, snarling, drawn-out cry that ended in a whine so piercing that Mr. Anderson's knees shook. One of the children, Violet Evelyn he thought, stirred in her bed and muttered: "Santa Claus! Santa Claus!" and Mr. Anderson, with a desperate effort, staggered on under his load and opened their door. The clock in the hall beneath began to strike twelve. Santa Claus, striving hard to appear jolly and genial, entered the room, and a huge grey, shadowy figure entered with him. A slipper thrown by Willie whizzed through the air, and, narrowly missing Santa Claus, fell to the ground with a clatter. There was then a deathly silence, and Violet and Horace, raising their heads, saw two strange figures standing in the centre of the room staring at one another—the one figure they at once identified by the costume. He was Santa Claus—but not the genial, rosy-cheeked Santa Claus their father had depicted. On the contrary, it was a Santa Claus with a very white face and frightened eyes—a Santa Claus that shook as if the snow and ice had given him the ague. But the other figure—what was it? Something very tall, far taller than their father, nude and grey, something like a man with the head of a wolf—a wolf with white pointed teeth and horrid, light eyes. Then they understood why it was that Santa Claus trembled; and Willie stood by the side of his bed, white and silent. It is impossible to say how long this state of things would have lasted, or what would eventually have happened, had not Mrs. Anderson, anxious to see how Santa Claus was faring, and rather wondering why he was gone so long, resolved herself to visit the children's room. As the light from her candle appeared on the threshold of the room the thing with the wolf's head vanished.

"Why, whatever were you all doing?" she began. Then Santa Claus and the children all spoke at once—whilst the sack of presents tumbled unheeded on the floor. Every available candle was soon lighted, and mother and father and Willie, Violet and Horace all spent the remainder of that night in close company. On the following day it was proposed, and carried unanimously, that the house should be put up for sale. This was done at the earliest opportunity, and fortunately for the Andersons suitable tenants were soon found. Before leaving, however, Mr. Anderson made another and more exhaustive search of the grounds, and discovered, in a cave in the hills immediately behind the house, a number of bones. Amongst them was the skull of a wolf, and lying close beside it a human skeleton, with only the skull missing. Mr. Anderson burnt the bones, hoping that by so doing he would rid the house of its unwelcome visitor; and, as his tenants so far have not complained, he believes that the hauntings have actually ceased.

A lady whom I met at Tavistock some years ago told me that she had seen a phantasm, which she believed to be that of a werwolf, in the Valley of the Doones, Exmoor. She was walking home alone, late one evening, when she saw on the path directly in front of her the tall grey figure of a man with a wolf's head. Advancing stealthily forward, this creature was preparing to spring on a large rabbit that was crouching on the ground, apparently too terror-stricken to move, when the abrupt appearance of a stag bursting through the bushes in a wild state of stampede caused it to vanish. Prior to this occurrence, my informant had never seen a ghost, nor had she, indeed, believed in them; but now, she assures me, she is quite convinced as to their existence, and is of the opinion that the sub-human phenomenon she had witnessed was the spirit of one of those werwolves referred to by Gervase of Tilbury and Richard Verstegan—werwolves who were still earthbound owing to their incorrigible ferocity.

This opinion I can readily endorse, adding only that, considering the number of werwolves there must once have been in England, it is a matter of some surprise to me that phantasms are not more frequently seen.

Here is another account of this type of haunting narrated to me some summers ago by a Mr. Warren, who at the time he saw the phenomenon was staying in the Hebrides, which part of the British Isles is probably richer than any other in spooks of all sorts.

"I was about fifteen years of age at the time," Mr. Warren said, "and had for several years been residing with my grandfather, who was an elder in the Kirk of Scotland. He was much interested in geology, and literally filled the house with fossils from the pits and caves round where we dwelt. One morning he came home in a great state of excitement, and made me go with him to look at some ancient remains he had found at the bottom of a dried-up tarn.

'Look!' he cried, bending down and pointing at them, 'here is a human skeleton with a wolf's head. What do you make of it?' I told him I did not know, but supposed it must be some kind of monstrosity. 'It's a werwolf!' he rejoined, 'that's what it is. A werwolf! This island was once overrun with satyrs and werwolves! Help me carry it to the house.' I did as he bid me, and we placed it on the table in the back kitchen. That evening I was left alone in the house, my grandfather and the other members of the household having gone to the kirk. For some time I amused myself reading, and then, fancying I heard a noise in the back premises, I went into the kitchen. There was no one about, and becoming convinced that it could only have been a rat that had disturbed me, I sat on the table alongside the alleged remains of the werwolf, and waited to see if the noises would recommence. I was thus waiting in a listless sort of way, my back bent, my elbows on my knees, looking at the floor and thinking of nothing in particular, when there came a loud rat, tat, tat of knuckles on the window-pane. I immediately turned in the direction of the noise and encountered, to my alarm, a dark face looking in at me. At first dim and indistinct, it became more and more complete, until it developed into a very perfectly defined head of a wolf terminating in the neck of a human being. Though greatly shocked, my first act was to look in every direction for a possible reflection—but in vain. There was no light either without or within, other than that from the setting sun—nothing that could in any way have produced an illusion. I looked at the face and marked each feature intently. It was unmistakably a wolf's face, the jaws slightly distended; the lips wreathed in a savage snarl; the teeth sharp and white; the eyes light green; the ears pointed. The expression of the face was diabolically malignant, and as it gazed straight at me my horror was as intense as my wonder. This it seemed to notice, for a look of savage exultation crept into its eyes, and it raised one hand—a slender hand, like that of a woman, though with prodigiously long and curved finger-nails—menacingly, as if about to dash in the window-pane. Remembering what my grandfather had told me about evil spirits, I crossed myself; but as this had no effect, and I really feared the thing would get at me, I ran out of the kitchen and shut and locked the door, remaining in the hall till the family returned. My grandfather was much upset when I told him what had happened, and attributed my failure to make the spirit depart to my want of faith. Had he been there, he assured me, he would soon have got rid of it; but he nevertheless made me help him remove the bones from the kitchen, and we reinterred them in the very spot where we had found them, and where, for aught I know to the contrary, they still lie."

The peasant class in all parts of the British Isles are so sensitive to ridicule, and so suspicious of being "got at," that it is very difficult to extract any information from them with regard to the superphysical. At first they invariably deny their belief in spirits, and it is only by dint of the utmost persuasion unaccompanied by any air of patronage—which the Celtic peasant detests—that one is finally able to loosen their tongues as to uncanny occurrences, hauntings, and rumours of hauntings, in their neighbourhood. In eliciting information of this nature, I have, I think, by reason of my tactful manner, often succeeded where others have failed.

In a village at the foot of Ben MacDhui a shepherd of the

name of Colin Graeme informed me that he remembered hearing his grandfather, who died at the age of ninety, speak of an old man called Tam McPherson whom he—the grandfather—had known intimately as a boy. This old man, so Colin's grandfather said, had perfect recollections of a man in the village called Saunderson being suspected of being a werwolf. He used to describe Saunderson as "a mon with evil, leerie eyes, and eyebrows that met in a point over his nose"; and went on to say that Saunderson lived in a cave in the mountains where his forefathers, also suspected of being werwolves, had lived before him, and that when on his—Saunderson's—death this cave was visited by some of the villagers, a quantity of queer bones—some human and some belonging to wolves—were discovered lying in corners, partially covered with stones and loose earth.

I have heard similar stories in Wales, and have been conducted to one or two spots, one near Tremadac and the other on the Epynt Hills, where, local tradition still has it, werwolves once flourished.

According to legend St. Patrick turned Vereticus, a Welsh king, into a wolf, whilst the werwolf daughter of a Welsh prince was said to have destroyed her father's enemies during her nocturnal metamorphoses. In Ireland, too, are many legends of werwolves; and it is said of at least some half-dozen of the old families that at some period—as the result of a curse—each member of the clan was doomed to be a wolf for seven years.

CHAPTER VII

# The Werwolf in France

IN NO COUNTRY has the werwolf flourished as in France, where it is known as the *loup garou*; where it has existed in all parts, in every age, and where it is even yet to be found in the more remote districts. Hence one could fill a dozen volumes with the stories, many of them well authenticated, of French werwolves. As far back as the sixth century we hear of them infesting the woods and valleys of Brittany and Burgundy, the Landes, and the mountainous regions of the Côte d'Or and the Cevennes.

Occasionally a werwolf would break into a convent and make its meal off the defenceless nuns; occasionally it would select for its repast some nice fat abbot waddling unsuspectingly home to his monastery.

Not all these werwolves were evilly disposed people; many, on the contrary, were exceedingly virtuous, and owed their metamorphosis to the vengeance of witch or wizard. When this was the case their piety sometimes prevailed to such an extent that not even metamorphosis into wolfish form could render it ineffective; and there are instances where werwolves of this type have not only refrained from taking human life, but have actually gone out of their way to protect it. Of such instances, well authenticated, probably none would be more remarkable than those I am about to narrate.

### THE CASE OF THE ABBOT GILBERT, OF THE ARC MONASTERY, ON THE BANKS OF THE LOIRE

Gilbert had been to a village fair, where the good vintage and hot sun combined had proved so trying that on his way home, through a dense and lonely forest, he had gone to sleep and been thrown from his horse. In falling he had bruised and cut himself so prodigiously that the blood from his wounds attracted to the spot a number of big wild cats. Taken at a strong disadvantage, and without any weapons to defend himself, Gilbert would soon have fallen a victim to the ferocity of these savage creatures had it not been for the opportune arrival of a werwolf. A desperate battle at once ensued, in which the werwolf eventually gained the victory, though not without being severely lacerated.

Despite Gilbert's protestations, for he was loath to be seen in such strange company, the werwolf accompanied him back to the monastery, where, upon hearing the Abbot's story, it was enthusiastically welcomed and its wounds attended to. At dawn it was restored to its natural shape, and the monks, one and all, were startled out of their senses to find themselves in the presence of a stern and awesome dignitary of the Church, who immediately began to lecture the Abbot for his unseemly conduct the previous day, ordering him to undergo such penance as eventually, robbing him of half his size and all his self-importance, led to his resignation.

## THE CASE OF ROLAND BERTIN

André Bonivon, the hero of the other incident, was eminently a man of war. He commanded a schooner called the "Bonaventure," which was engaged in harassing the Huguenot settlements along the shores of the Gulf of Lions, during the reign of Louis XIV. On one of his marauding expeditions Bonivon sailed up an estuary of the Rhone rather further than he had intended, and having no pilot on board, ran ashore in the darkness. A thunderstorm came on; a general panic ensued; and Bonivon soon found himself struggling in a whirlpool. Powerful swimmer though he was, he would most certainly have been drowned had not some one come to his assistance, and, freeing him from the heavy clothes which weighed him down, dragged him on dry land. The moment Bonivon got on *terra firma*, sailor-like, he extended his hand to grip that of his rescuer, when, to his dismay and terror, instead of a hand he grasped a huge hairy paw.

Convinced that he was in the presence of the Devil, who doubtless highly approved of the thousand and one atrocities he had perpetrated on the helpless Huguenots, he threw himself on his knees and implored the forgiveness of Heaven.

His rescuer waited awhile in grim silence, and then, lifting him gently to his feet, led him some considerable distance inland till they arrived at a house on the outskirts of a small town.

Here Bonivon's conductor halted, and, opening the door, signed to the captain to enter. All within was dark and silent, and the air was tainted with a sickly, pungent odour that filled Bonivon with the gravest apprehensions. Dragging him along, Bonivon's guide took him into a room, and leaving him there for some seconds, reappeared carrying a lantern. Bonivon now saw for the first time the face of his conductor—it was that of a werwolf. With a shriek of terror Bonivon turned to run, but, catching his foot on a mat, fell sprawling on the floor.

Here he remained sobbing and shaking with fear till he was once more taken by the werwolf and set gently on his feet.

To Bonivon's surprise a tray full of eatables was standing on the table, and the werwolf, motioning to him to sit down, signed to him to eat.

Being ravenously hungry, Bonivon "fell to," and, despite his fears—for being by nature alive to, and, by reason of his calling, forced to guard against the treachery of his fellow creatures, he more than half suspected some subtle design underlying this act of kindness—demolished every particle of food. The meal thus concluded, Bonivon's benefactor retired, locking the door after him.

No sooner had the sound of his steps in the stone hall ceased than Bonivon ran to the window, hoping thereby to make his escape. But the iron bars were too firmly fixed—no matter how hard he pulled, tugged and wrenched, they remained as immovable as ever. Then his heart began to palpitate, his hair to bristle up, and his knees to totter; his thoughts were full of speculations as to how he would be killed and what it would feel like to be eaten alive. His conscience, too, rising up in judgment against him, added its own paroxysms of dismay, paroxysms which were still further augmented by the finding of the dead body of a woman, nude and horribly mutilated, lying doubled up and partly concealed by a curtain. Such a discovery could not fail to fill his heart with unspeakable horror; for he concluded that he himself, unless saved by a miracle—a favour he could hardly hope for, considering his past conduct—would undergo the same fate before morning. At a loss to know what else to do, he sat upon the corner of the table, resting his chin on the palms of his hands, and engaged in anticipations of the most frightful nature.

Shortly after dawn he heard the sound of footsteps approaching the room; the door slowly began to open: a little wider and a little wider, and then, when Bonivon's heart was on the point of bursting, it suddenly swung open wide, and the cold, grey dawn falling on the threshold revealed not a werwolf, but—a human being: a man in the unmistakable garb of a Huguenot minister!

The reaction was so great that Bonivon rolled off the table and went into paroxysms of ungovernable laughter.

At length, when he had sobered down, the Huguenot, laying a hand on his shoulder, said: "Do you know now where you are? Do you recognize this room? No! Well, I will explain. You are in the house of Roland Bertin, and the body lying over yonder is that of my wife, whom your crew barbarously murdered yesterday when they sacked this village. They took me with them, and it was your intention to have me tortured and then drowned as soon as you got to sea. Do you know me now?"

Bonivon nodded—he could not have spoken to save his life.

"Bien!" the minister went on. "I am a werwolf—I was bewitched some years ago by the woman Grénier, Mère Grénier, who lives in the forest at the back of our village. As soon as it was dark I metamorphosed; then the ship ran ashore, and every one leaped overboard. I saw you drowning. I saved you."

The captain again made a fruitless effort to speak, and the Huguenot continued:—

"Why did I save you?—you, who had been instrumental in murdering my wife and ruining my home! Why? I do not know! Had I preferred for you a less pleasant death than drowning, I could have taken you ashore and killed you. Yet—I did not, because it is not in my nature to destroy anything. I have never in my life killed an animal, nor, to my knowledge, an insect; I love all life—animal life and vegetable life—everything that breathes and grows. Yet I am a Huguenot!—one of the race you hate and despise and are paid to exterminate. Assassin, I have spared you. Be not ungenerous. Spare others."

The captain was moved. Still speechless, he seized the minister's hands and wrung them. And from that hour to the day of his death—which was not for many years afterwards—the Huguenots had no truer friend than André Bonivon.

## WERWOLVES AND WITCHES

Other instances of werwolves of a benignant nature are to be found in the "Bisclaveret" in Marie de France's poem, composed in 1200 a.d.; and in the hero of "William and the Werwolf" (translated from the French about 1350).

To inflict the evil property of werwolfery upon those against whom they—or some other—bore a grudge was, in the Middle Ages, a method of revenge frequently resorted to by witches; and countless knights and ladies were thus victimized. Nor were such practices confined to ancient times; for as late as the eighteenth century a case of this kind of witchcraft is reported to have happened in the vicinity of Blois.

In a village some three miles from Blois, on the outskirts of a forest, dwelt an innkeeper called Antonio Cellini, who, as the name suggests, was of Italian origin. Antonio had only one child, Beatrice, a very pretty girl, who at the time of this story was about nineteen years of age. As might be expected, Beatrice had many admirers; but none were so passionately attached to her as Herbert Poyer, a handsome youth, and one Henri Sangfeu, an extremely plain youth. Beatrice—and one can scarcely blame her for it—preferred Herbert, and with the whole-hearted approval of her father consented to marry him. Sangfeu was not unnaturally upset; but, in all probability, he would have eventually resigned himself to the inevitable, had it not been for a village wag, who in an idle moment wrote a poem and entitled it "*Sansfeu the Ugly; or, Love Unrequited.*"

The poem, which was illustrated with several clever caricatures of the unfortunate Henri and contained much caustic wit, took like wildfire in the village; and Henri, in consequence, had a very bad time. Eventually it was shown to Beatrice, and it was then that the climax was reached. Although Henri was present at the moment, unable to restrain herself, she went into peals of laughter at the drawings, saying over and over again: "How like him—how very like! His nose to a nicety! It is certainly correct to style him Sansfeu—for no one could call him Sansnez!"

Her mirth was infectious; every one joined in; only Henri slunk away, crimson with rage and mortification. He hated Beatrice now as much as he had loved her before; and he thirsted only for revenge.

Some distance from the village and in the heart of the forest lived an old woman known as Mère Maxim, who was said to be a witch, and, therefore, shunned by every one. All sorts of unsavoury stories were told of her, and she was held responsible for several outbreaks of epidemics—hitherto unknown in the neighbourhood—many accidents, and more than one death.

The spot where she lived was carefully avoided. Those who ventured far in the forest after nightfall either never came back at all or returned half imbecile with terror, and afterwards poured out to their affrighted friends incoherent stories of the strange lights and terrible forms they had encountered, moving about amid the trees. Up to the present Henri had been just as scared by these tales as the rest of the villagers; but so intense was his longing for revenge that he at length resolved to visit Mère Maxim and solicit her assistance. Choosing a morning when the sun was shining brightly, he screwed up his courage, and after many bad scares finally succeeded in reaching her dwelling—or, I might say, her shanty, for by a more appropriate term than the latter such a queer-looking untidy habitation could not be described. To his astonishment Mère Maxim was by no means so unprepossessing as he had imagined. On the contrary, she was more than passably good-looking, with black hair, rosy cheeks, and exceedingly white teeth. What he did not altogether like were her eyes—which, though large and well shaped, had in them an occasional glitter—and her hands, which, though remarkably white and slender, had very long and curved nails, that to his mind suggested all sorts of unpleasant ideas. She was becomingly dressed in brown—brown woolly garments, with a brown fur cap, brown stockings, and brown shoes ornamented with very bright silver buckles. Altogether she was decidedly chic; and if a little incongruous in her surroundings, such incongruity only made her the more alluring; and as far as Henri was concerned rather added to her charms.

At all events, he needed no second invitation to seat himself by her side in the chimney-corner, and his heart thumped as it had never thumped before when she encouraged him to put his arm round her waist and kiss her. It was the first time a woman had ever suffered him to kiss her without violent protestations and avowals of disgust.

"You are not very handsome, it is true," Mère Maxim remarked, "but you are fat— and I like fat young men," and she pinched his cheeks playfully and patted his hands. "Are you sure no one knows you have come to see me?" she asked.

"Certain!" Henri replied; "I haven't confided in a soul; I haven't even so much as dropped a hint that I intended seeing you."

"That is good!" Mère Maxim said. "Tell no one, otherwise I shall not be able to help you. Also, on no account let the girl Beatrice think you bear her animosity. Be civil and friendly to her whenever you meet; then give her, as a wedding present, this belt and box of bonbons." So saying, she handed him a beautiful belt composed of the skin of some wild animal and fastened with a gold buckle, and a box of delicious pink and white sugarplums. "Do not give her these things till the marriage eve," she added, "and directly you have given them come and see me—always observing the greatest secrecy." She then kissed him, and he went away brimming over with passion for her, and longing feverishly for the hour to arrive when he could be with her again.

All day and all night he thought of her—of her gay and sparkling beauty, of her kisses and caresses, and the delightful coolness of her thin and supple hands. His mad infatuation for her made him oblivious to the taunts and jeers of the villagers, who seldom saw him without making ribald allusion to the poem.

"There goes Sansfeu! alias Monsieur Grosnez!" they called out. "Why don't you cut off your nose for a present to mademoiselle? She would then have no need to buy a kitchen poker. Ha! ha! ha!" But their coarse wit fell flat. Henri hardly heard it—all his thoughts, his burning love, his unquenchable passion, were centred in Mère Maxim: in spirit he was with her, alone with her, in the innermost recesses of the grim, silent forest.

The marriage eve came; he handed Beatrice the presents, and ere she had time to thank him—for the magnificence of the belt rendered her momentarily speechless—he had flown from the house, and was hurrying as fast as his legs could carry him to his tryst. The shadows of night were already on the forest when he entered it; and the silence and solitude of the place, the indistinct images of the trees, and their dismal sighing, that seemed to foretell a storm, all combined to disturb his fancy and raise strange spectres in his imagination. The shrill hooting of an owl, as it rustled overhead, caused him an unprecedented shock, and the great rush of blood to his head made him stagger and clutch hold of the nearest object for support. He had barely recovered from this alarm when his eyes almost started out of their sockets with fright as he caught sight of a queer shape gliding silently from tree to tree; and shortly afterwards he was again terrified—this time by a pale face, whether of a human being or animal he could not say, peering down at him from the gnarled and fantastic branches of a gigantic oak. He was now so frightened that he ran, and queer—indefinably queer footsteps ran after him, and followed him persistently until he reached the shanty, when he heard them turn and leap lightly away.

On this occasion, the occurrence of Henri's second visit, Mère Maxim was more captivating than ever. She was dressed with wonderful effect all in white. She wore sparkling jewels at her throat and waist, buckles of burnished gold on her shoes; her teeth flashed like polished ivory, and her nails like agates. Henri was enraptured. He fell on his knees before her, he caught her hands and covered them with kisses.

"How nice you look to-day, my sweetheart," she said; "and how fat! It does my heart good to see you. Come in, and sit close to me, and tell me how you have fared."

She led him in, and after locking and barring the door, conducted him to the chimney-corner. And there he lay in her arms. She fondled him; she pressed her lips on his, and gleefully felt his cheeks and arms. And after a time, when, intoxicated with the joy of it all, he lay still and quiet, wishing only to remain like that for eternity, she stooped down, and, fetching a knot of cord from under the seat, began laughingly to bind his hands and feet. And at each turn and twist of the rope she laughed the louder. And when she had finished binding his arms and legs she made him lie on his back, and lashed him so tightly to the seat that, had he possessed the strength of six men, he could not have freed himself.

Then she sat beside him, and moving aside the clothes that covered his chest and throat, said:—

"By this time Beatrice—pretty Beatrice, vain and sensual Beatrice, the Beatrice you once loved and admired so much—will have worn the belt, will have eaten the sweets. She is now a werwolf. Every night at twelve o'clock she will creep out of bed and glide about the house and village in search of human prey, some bonny babe, or weak, defenceless woman, but always some one fat, tender, and juicy—some one like you." And bending low over him, she bared her teeth, and dug her cruel nails deep into his flesh. A flame from the wood fire suddenly shot up. It flickered oddly on the figure of Mère Maxim—so oddly that Henri received a shock. He realized with an awful thrill that the face into which he peered was no longer that of a human being; it was—but he could no longer think—he could only gaze.

## CHAPTER VIII

# Werwolves and Vampires and Ghouls

THROUGHOUT THE MIDDLE AGES, and even in the seventeenth century, trials for lycanthropy were of common occurrence in France. Among the most famous were those of the Grandillon family in the Jura, in 1598; that of the tailor of Châlons; of Roulet, in Angers; of Gilles Garnier, in Dôle, in 1573; and of Jean Garnier, at Bordeaux, in 1603. The last case was, perhaps, the most remarkable of all. Garnier, who was only fourteen years of age, was employed in looking after cattle. He was a handsome lad, with dark, flashing eyes and very white teeth. As soon as it was time for the metamorphosis to take place he used to go into some lonely spot, and then, in the guise of a wolf, return, and run to earth isolated women and children. One of his favourite haunts was a thicket close to a pool of water. Here he used to lie and watch for hours at a time. Once he surprised two girls bathing. One escaped, and fled home naked, but the other he flung on the ground, and having shaken her into submission, devoured a portion of her one day, and the rest of her the next. He confessed to having eaten over fifty children. Nor did he always confine himself to attacking the solitary few and defenceless; for on several occasions, when hard pressed by hunger, he assailed a whole crowd, and was once severely handled by a pack of young girls who successfully drove him off with sharply pointed stakes. Far from wishing to conceal his guilt, Jean Garnier was most eager to tell everything, and to a court thronged with eager, attentive people, he related in the most graphic manner possible his sanguinary experiences. One old woman, he said, whom he found alone in a cottage, showed extraordinary agility in trying to escape. She raced round tables, clambered over chairs, crawled under a bed, and finally hid in a cupboard and held the door so fast that he had to exert all his force to open it. "And then," he added, "in spite of all my trouble she proved to be as tough as leather——" and he made a grimace that provoked much laughter.

He complained bitterly of one child. "It made such a dreadful noise," he said, "when I lifted it out of its crib, and when I got ready for my first bite it shrieked so loud it almost deafened me."

The name Grénier, like that of Garnier, was closely associated with lycanthropy, and in Blois, where there were more instances of lycanthropy than in any other part of France, every one called Grénier or Garnier was set down as a werwolf.

Amongst the Vaudois lycanthropy was also widely prevalent, and many of these werwolves were brought to trial and executed.

## THE CASE OF SERGEANT BERTRAND

The case of Sergeant Bertrand, which is the last authenticated case of this kind, occurred in 1847, when, on the 10th of July, an investigation was held before a military council presided over by Colonel Manselon. For some months the cemeteries in and around Paris had been the scenes of frightful violations, the culprits (or culprit), in some extraordinary manner, eluding every attempt made to ensnare them. At one time the custodians of the cemeteries were suspected, then the local police, and for a brief space suspicion fell even on the relations of the dead. The first burial-place to be so mysteriously visited was the Cemetery of Père Lachaise. Here, at night, those in charge declared they saw a strange form, partly human and partly animal, glide about from tomb to tomb. Try how they would they could not catch it—it always vanished—vanished just like a phantom directly they came up to it; and the dogs when urged to seize it would only bark and howl, and show indications of the most abject terror.

Always when morning broke the ravages of this unsavoury visitant were only too plainly visible—graves had been dug up, coffins burst open, and the contents nibbled, and gnawed, and scattered all over the ground. Expert medical opinion was sought, but with no fresh result. The doctors, too, were agreed that the mutilations of the dead were produced by the bites of what certainly seemed to be human teeth.

The sensation caused by this announcement was without parallel; and one and all, old and young, rich and poor, were wanting to know whatever sort of being it could be that possessed so foul an appetite. The watch was doubled; all to no purpose. A young soldier was arrested, but on declaring he had merely entered the cemetery to meet a friend, and exhibiting no evidences of guilt, was let go.

At length the violation ceased in Père Lachaise and broke out elsewhere. A little girl, greatly beloved by her relatives and friends, died, and a big concourse of people attended the funeral. On the following morning, to the intense indignation of every one, the grave was discovered dug up, the coffin forced open, and the body half eaten. In its wild fury at such an unheard-of atrocity the public called loudly for the culprit. The father of the dead girl was first of all arrested, but his innocence being quickly established, he was set free. Every means was then taken to guard against any recurrence, but in spite of all precautions the same thing happened again shortly afterwards; and happened repeatedly. The fact that the cemetery was surrounded by very high walls, and that iron gates, which were always kept shut, formed the only legitimate entrance, added to the mystery, and made it seem impossible that any creature of solid flesh and blood could be responsible for the outrages.

Having observed that at one place, in particular, the wall, though nearly ten feet high, showed signs of having been frequently scaled, an old army officer set a trap there, consisting of a wire connected with an explosive, which was so arranged that no one could climb over the wall without treading on the wire and causing an explosion.

A strong posse of detectives kept watch, and at midnight a loud report was heard. The detectives were not, however, as quick as their quarry. They saw a man, or what they took to be a man, and fired at him, but he was gone like a flash of lightning, scaling the wall with the agility of a monkey. Finding a trail of blood, however, and pieces of torn uniform accompanying the bloodstains, they concluded that the enemy was wounded, and that the marauder was, moreover, a soldier.

Still, it is doubtful whether his identity would have been proved, had not one of the grave-diggers of the cemetery chanced to overhear some sappers of the 74th Regiment remark that on the preceding night one of their comrades—a sergeant—had been conveyed to the military hospital of Val de Grâce badly wounded. The matter was at once inquired into, and the wounded soldier, Sergeant Bertrand, was found to be the author of the long series of hideous violations. Bertrand freely confessed his guilt, declaring that he was driven to it against his own will by some external force he could not define, and which allowed him no peace. He had, he said, in one night exhumed and bitten as many as fifteen bodies. He employed no implements, but tore up the soil after the manner of a wild beast, paying no heed to the bruising and laceration of his hands so long as he could get at the dead. He could not describe what his sensations were like when he was thus occupied; he only knew that he was not himself but some ravenous, ferocious animal. He added, that after these nocturnal expeditions he invariably fell into a profound sleep, often before he could get home, and that always, during that sleep, he was conscious of undergoing peculiar metamorphosis. When interrogated, he informed the court of inquiry that, as a child, he preferred the company of all kinds of animals to that of his fellow creatures, and that in order to get in close touch with his four-footed friends he used to frequent the most solitary and out-of-the-way places—moors, woods, and deserts. He said that it was immediately after one of these excursions that he first experienced the sensation of undergoing some great change in his sleep, and that the following evening, when passing close to a cemetery where the grave-diggers were covering a body that had just been interred, yielding to a sudden impulse, he crept in and watched them. A sharp shower of rain interrupting their labours, they went away, leaving their task unfinished. "At the sight of the coffin," Bertrand said, "horrible desires seized me; my head throbbed, my heart palpitated, and had it not been for the timely arrival of friends I should have then and there yielded to my inclinations. From that time forth I was never free—these terrible cravings invariably came on directly after sunset."

Medical men who examined Bertram unanimously gave it as their opinion that he was sane, and could only account for his extraordinary nocturnal actions by the supposition that he must be the victim of some strange monomania. His companions, with whom he was most popular, all testified to his amiability and lovable disposition. In the end he was sentenced to a year's imprisonment, and after his release was never again heard of. There can, I think, be little doubt, from what he himself said, that he was in reality a werwolf. His preference for the society of animals and love of isolated regions; his sudden fallings asleep and sensations of undergoing metamorphosis, though that metamorphosis was spiritual and metaphysical only, which is very often the case, all help to substantiate that belief.

## VAMPIRISM AND LYCANTHROPY

It has been asserted that Bertrand was a vampire; but there are absolutely no grounds for associating him with vampirism. A vampire is an Elemental that under certain conditions inhabits a dead body, whether human or otherwise; and, thus incarcerated, comes out of a grave at night to suck the blood of a living person. It never touches the dead.

A werwolf has already been defined. It has an existence entirely separate from the vampire. The werwolf feeds on both the living and dead, which it bites and mangles after the nature of all beasts of prey.

Vampirism is infectious; every one who has been sucked by a vampire, on physical dissolution, becomes a vampire, and remains one until his corpse is destroyed in a certain prescribed manner. Lycanthropy is not infectious.

There are many well-authenticated cases of vampirism in France and Germany. In a newspaper published in the reign of Louis XV there appeared an announcement to the effect that Arnold Paul, a native of Madveiga, being crushed to death by a wagon and buried, had since become a vampire, and that he had been previously bitten by one. The authorities being informed of the terror his visits were occasioning, and several people having died with all the symptoms of vampirism, his grave was opened; and although he had been dead forty days his body was like that of a very full-blooded, living man.

Following the mode of exorcism traditionally observed on such occasions, a stake was driven into the corpse, whereupon it uttered a frightful cry—half human and half animal; after which its head was cut off, and trunk and head burned. Four other bodies which had died from the consequences of the bites, and which were found in the same perfectly healthy condition, were served in a similar manner; and it was hoped these vigorous measures would end the mischief.

But no such thing; cases of deaths from the same cause—*i.e.*, loss of blood—still continued, and five years afterwards became so rife that the authorities were compelled to take the matter up for the second time. On this occasion the graves of many people, of all ages and both sexes, were opened, and the bodies of all those suspected of plaguing the living by their nocturnal visits were found in the vampire state—full almost to overflowing with blood, and free from every symptom of death. On their being served in the same manner as the corpse of Arnold Paul the epidemic of vampirism ceased, and no more cases of it have since been reported as occurring in that district. A rumour of these proceedings reaching the ears of Louis XV, he at once ordered his Minister at Vienna to report upon them. This was done. The documents forwarded to the King (and which are still in existence) give a detailed account of all the occurrences to which I have referred. They bear the date of June 7, 1732, and are signed and witnessed by three surgeons and several other persons.

The facts, which are indubitable, point to no other satisfactory explanation saving that of vampirism—an explanation that finds ample corroboration in thousands of like cases reported, at one time or another, in every country in Eastern Europe.

## GHOULISM AND LYCANTHROPY

Sergeant Bertrand has also been declared a ghoul. Ghoulism bears a somewhat closer resemblance than vampirism to lycanthropy. A ghoul is an Elemental that visits any place where human or animal remains have been interred. It digs them up and bites them, showing a keen liking for brains, which it sucks in the same manner as a vampire sucks blood.

Ghouls either remain in spirit form or steal the bodies of living beings—living beings only—either human or animal. They can only do this when the spirit of the living person, during sleep (either natural or induced hypnotically), is separated from the material body; or, in other words, when the spirit is projected. The ghoul then pounces on the physical body, and, often refusing to restore it to its rightful owner, the latter is compelled to roam about as a phantasm for just so long a time as the ghoul chooses to inhabit the body it has stolen.

## THE CASE OF CONSTANCE ARMANDE, GHOUL

*À propos* of ghouls, the following incident was related to me as having occurred recently in Brittany. A young girl named Constance Armande, in a good station of life, much against the wishes of her family, took up spiritualism and constantly attended séances. At these séances she witnessed all sorts of phenomena—some in all probability produced by mere trickery on the part of the medium or a confederate, whilst others were, without doubt, the manifestations of *bona fide* spirits—earthbound phantasms of the lowest and most undesirable order—murderers, lunatics, Vice Elementals, and ghouls. It is most unwise to risk coming in contact with such spirits, for when they have once made your acquaintance they will attach themselves to you, and are got rid of only with the greatest difficulty. They were most unremitting in their persecution of Constance Armande; they followed her home, and were always rapping on the walls of her room and disturbing and annoying her. In short, she got no peace, either asleep or awake. In the night she would often wake up screaming, and in an agony of mind rush into her parents' room and implore their protection, declaring she had dreamed in the most vivid manner possible that frightful-looking creatures, too awful for her to describe, were trying to prevent her awaking in order to keep her with them always. She told a spiritualist, and he informed her that such dreams were not in reality dreams at all, but projections—that she had, at séances, acquired the power of projection; and, having no control over that power, she projected herself unconsciously, the projection almost always taking place in her sleep.

A medical expert was also consulted, and in accordance with his advice Constance Armande went to the seaside and resorted to every kind of pleasure—balls, concerts, and theatres. But the annoyances still continued, and she was seldom permitted to rest a whole night without being disturbed in a most harrowing manner.

Being a really beautiful girl, she had countless admirers, and eventually she became engaged to Alphonse Mabane, the only son of a very wealthy widow.

Shortly before the day fixed for their marriage Madame Mabane was seized with a fit of apoplexy and died. Every one, especially Constance Armande, was overwhelmed with grief, whilst preparations were made for a most impressive funeral.

On the afternoon of the day preceding that on which the funeral was to take place Constance, complaining of a bad headache, went to lie down on her bed, and two hours later strange footsteps were heard coming out of her room and bounding down the stairs.

Wondering who it could be, Madame Armande ran to look, and was astonished beyond measure to see Constance—but a Constance she hardly knew—a Constance with the glitter of a ferocious beast in her eyes, and a grim, savage expression in the corners of her mouth. She did not appear to notice her mother, but passed her by with a light, stealthy tread, utterly unlike her usual walk, crossed the hall, and went out at the front door. Madame Armande was too startled to try and intercept her, or even to make any remark, and returned to the drawing-room greatly agitated. As hour after hour passed and Constance did not come home, her alarm increased, and she mentioned the incident to her husband, who caused immediate inquiries to be made. Just about the hour the family usually retired to rest there came a violent ring at the front-door bell. It was Alphonse Mabane, pale and ghastly.

"Have you found her?" Monsieur and Madame Armande cried, catching hold of him in their agitation, and dragging him into the hall.

Alphonse nodded. "Let me sit down a moment first," he gasped. "It will give me time to collect my senses. My nerves are all to pieces!"

He sank into a chair, and, burying his face in his hands, shook convulsively. Monsieur and Madame Armande stood and watched him in agonized silence. After some minutes—to the Armandes it seemed an eternity—spent in this fashion, Alphonse raised his head. "Your servant," he said, "came to my house at nine o'clock and asked if Mademoiselle Constance was with me. I said 'No,' that I had not seen her all day, and was much alarmed when I was informed that she had left home early in the afternoon and had not yet returned. I said I would join in the search for her, and was in my bedroom putting on my overcoat, when there came a tap at my door, and Jacques, my valet, with a face as white as a sheet, begged me to go with him upstairs. He led me to the door of my mother's room, where she lay in her coffin, not yet screwed down. 'Hark!' he whispered, touching me on the sleeve, 'do you hear that?'

"I listened, and from the interior of the room came a curious noise like munching—a steady gnaw, gnaw, gnaw. 'I heard it just now,' he whispered, 'when I was going to shut the landing window—and other sounds, too. Hush!'

"I held my breath, and heard distinctly the swishing and rustling of a dress.

"'Have you been in?' I asked.

"He shook his head. 'I daren't,' he whispered. 'I wouldn't go in by myself if you were to offer me a million pounds,' and he trembled so violently that he had to lean against me for support.

"A great terror then seized me, and bidding Jacques follow, I crept downstairs and summoned the rest of the servants. Armed with sticks and lights, we then went in a body to my mother's room, and throwing open the door, rushed in.

"The lid of the coffin was off, the corpse was lying huddled up on the floor, and crouching over it was Constance. For God's sake don't ask me to describe more—the sounds we heard explained everything. When she saw us she emitted a series of savage snarls, sprang at one of the maids, scratched her in the face, and before we could stop her, flew downstairs and out into the street. As soon as our shocked senses had sufficiently recovered we started off in pursuit, but have not been able to find the slightest trace of her."

At the conclusion of Monsieur Mabane's story the search was continued. The police were summoned, and a general hue and cry raised, with the result that Constance was eventually found in a cemetery digging frantically at a newly made grave.

At last brought to bay in the chase that ensued, fortunately for her and for all concerned, she plunged into a river, was swept away by the current, and drowned.

This case of Constance Armande seems to me to be clearly a case of ghoulism. What the spiritualist had told her was correct—she had projected herself unconsciously, and the hideous things she imagined were phantoms in a dream were Elementals—ghouls—her projected spirit encountered on the superphysical plane.

After sundry efforts to steal her body when she was thus separated from it, one of them had at length succeeded, and, incarcerated in her beautiful frame, had hastened to satisfy its craving for human carrion.

# CHAPTER IX
# Werwolves in Germany

NO COUNTRY IN the world is richer in stories of everything appertaining to the supernatural than Germany. The Rhine is the favourite river of nymphs and sirens, to whose irresistible and fatal fascinations so many men have fallen victims. Along its shores are countless haunted castles, in its woods innumerable terrifying phantoms.

The werwolf, however, seems to have confined itself almost entirely to the Harz Mountains, where it was formerly most common and more dreaded than any other visitant from the Unknown. But of these werwolves many of the best authenticated cases have been told so often, that it is difficult for me to alight on any that is not already well known. Perhaps the following, though as striking as any, may be new to at least a few of my readers.

## THE CASE OF HERR HELLEN AND THE WERWOLVES OF THE HARZ MOUNTAINS

Two gentlemen, named respectively Hellen and Schiller, were on a walking tour in the Harz Mountains, in the early summer of the year

1840, when Schiller, slipping down, sprained his ankle and was unable to go on. They were some miles from any village, in the centre of an extensive forest, and it was beginning to get dark.

"Leave me here," cried the injured man to his friend, "while you see if you can discover any habitation. I have been told these woods are full of charcoal-burners' and wood-cutters' huts, so that if you walk straight ahead for a mile or two, you are very likely to come across one. Do go, there's a good fellow, and if you are too tired to return yourself, send some one to carry me."

Hellen did not like leaving his comrade in such a dreary spot, alone and helpless, but as Schiller was persistent he at length yielded, and stepping briskly out, advanced along the track that had brought them hither. Once or twice he halted, fancying he heard voices, and several times his heart pulsated wildly at what he took to be the cry of a wolf—for neither Schiller nor he had no weapons excepting sheath-knives. At last he came to an open spot hedged in on all sides by gloomy pines, the shadows from which were beginning to fall thick and fast athwart the vivid greensward. It was one of those places—they are to be found in pretty nearly every country—studiously avoided by local woodsmen as the haunt of all manner of evil influences. Hellen recognized it as such the moment he saw it, but as it lay right across his path, and time was pressing, he had no alternative but to keep boldly on. He was half-way across the spot when he was startled by a groan, and looking in the direction of the sound, he saw a man seated on the ground endeavouring to bandage his hand. Wondering why he had not observed him before, but thankful to meet some one at last, Hellen went up to him and asked what was the matter.

"I've broken my wrist," the man replied. "I was gathering sticks for my fire to-morrow when I heard the howl of a wolf, and in my anxiety to escape a conflict with the brute I climbed this tree. As I descended one of the branches gave way, and I fell down with all my weight on my right arm. Will you see if you can bind it for me? I'm a bit awkward with my left hand."

"I will do my best," Hellen said, and kneeling beside the man, he took off the bandages and wrapped them round again. "There," he exclaimed, "I think that is better—at least it is the best I can do."

The stranger was now most profuse in his thanks, and when Hellen informed him of Schiller's condition, at once cried out, "You must both come to my cottage; it is only a short distance from here. Let us hasten thither now, and my daughter, who is very strong, shall go back with you and help you carry your friend. We are not rich, but we can make you both fairly comfortable, and all we have shall be at your disposal. But I wonder if you know what you have incurred by coming to this spot at this hour?"

"Why, no," Hellen said, laughing. "What?"

"The gratification of two wishes—the first two wishes you make! Of course, you will say it is all humbug, but, believe me, very queer things do happen in this forest. I have experienced them myself."

"Well!" Hellen replied, laughing more heartily than before, "if I wish anything at all it is that my wife were here to see how beautifully I have bandaged your wrist."

"Where is your wife?" the stranger inquired.

"At Frankfort, most likely taking a final peep at the children in bed before retiring to rest herself!" Hellen said, still laughing.

"Then you have children!" the stranger ejaculated, evidently interested.

"Yes, three—all girls—and such bonny girls, too. Marcella, Christina, and Fredericka. I wish I had them here for you to see."

"I should much like to see them, certainly," the stranger said. "And now you have told me so much of interest about yourself, let me tell you something of my own history in exchange. My name is Wilfred Gaverstein. I am an artist by profession, and have come to live here during the summer months in order to paint nature—nature as it really is—in all its varying moods. Nature is my only god—I adore it. I don't believe in souls. I love the trees and flowers and shrubs, the rivulets, the fountains, the birds and insects."

"Everything but the wolves!" Hellen remarked jocularly. Hardly, however, had he spoken these words before he had reason to alter his tone. "Great heavens! do you hear that?" he cried. "There is no mistake about it this time. It is a wolf, or may I never live to hear one again."

"You are right, friend," Wilfred said. "It is a wolf, and not very far away, either. Come, we must be quick," and thrusting his arm through that of Hellen, he hurried him along. After some minutes' fast walking they came in sight of a neatly thatched whitewashed cottage, at the entrance to which two women and several children were collected. "That's my home," Wilfred said.

"And that's my wife!" Hellen cried, rubbing his eyes to make sure he was not dreaming. "God in heaven, what's the meaning of it all? My wife and children—all three of them! Am I mad?"

"It is merely the answer to your wishes," Wilfred rejoined calmly. "See, they recognize you and are waving."

As one in a sleep Hellen now staggered forward, and was soon in the midst of his family, who, rushing up to him, implored him to explain what had happened, and how on earth they came to be there.

"I am just as much at sea as you are," Hellen said, feeling them each in turn to make sure it was really they. "It's an insoluble mystery to me."

"And to us, too," they all cried. "A few minutes ago we were in our beds in Frankfort, and then suddenly we found ourselves here—here in this dreadful looking forest. Oh, take us away, take us home, do!"

Hellen was in despair. It was all like a hideous nightmare to him. What was he to do?

"You must be my guests for to-night, at all events," Wilfred said; "and in the morning we will discuss what is to be done. Fortunately we have enough room to accommodate you all. There is food in abundance. Let me introduce you to my daughter Marguerite," and the next moment Hellen found himself shaking hands with a girl of about twenty years of age. She was clad in what appeared to be a travelling dress, deeply bordered with white fur, and wore a most becoming cap of white ermine. Her feet were shod in long, pointed, and very elegant buckskin shoes, adorned with bright silver buckles. Her hair, which was yellow and glossy, was parted down the middle, and waved in a most becoming fashion low over the forehead and ears; and her features—at least so Hellen thought—were very beautiful. Her mouth, though a trifle large, had very daintily cut lips, and was furnished with unusually white and even teeth. But there was a peculiar furtive expression in her eyes, which were of a very pretty shape and colour, that aroused Hellen's curiosity, and made him scrutinize her carefully. Her hands were noticeably long and slender, with tapering fingers and long, almond-shaped, rosy nails, that glittered each time they caught the rays of the fast fading sunlight. Hellen's first impression of her was that she was marvellously beautiful, but that there was a something about her that he did not understand—a something he had never seen in anyone before, a something that in an ugly woman might have put him on his guard, but in this face of such surpassing beauty a something he seemed only too ready to ignore. Hellen was a good, and up to the present, certainly, a faithful husband, but he was only a man after all, and the more he looked at the girl the more he admired her.

At a word from Wilfred, Marguerite smilingly led the way indoors, and showed the guests two bedrooms, small but exquisitely clean. There was a double bed in one, and two single ones in the other. The bed-linen was of the very finest material, and white as snow.

"I think," Wilfred remarked, "two of the girls can squeeze in one bed—they are neither of them very big—though it does my heart good to see them so bonny."

"And mine, too," Marguerite joined in, patting the three children on the cheeks in turn, and drawing them to her and caressing them.

Mrs. Hellen, still dazed, and apparently hardly realizing what was happening, stammered out her thanks, and the party then descended to the kitchen to partake of a substantial supper that was speedily prepared for them.

"Had you not better go and look for your friend now?" Wilfred observed, just as Hellen was about to seat himself beside his wife and children. "Marguerite will go with you, and on your return the three of you can have your meal in here after the children have gone to bed."

Hellen readily assented, and kissing his wife and little ones, who tearfully implored him not to be gone long, set out, accompanied by Marguerite.

At each step they took, Marguerite's beauty became more irresistible. The soft rays of the moon falling directly on her features enhanced their loveliness, and Hellen could not keep his eyes off her. The ominous cry of a night bird startled her; she edged timidly up to him; and he had to exert all his self-control, so eager was he to clasp her to him. In a strained, unnatural manner he kept up a flow of small-talk, eliciting the information that she was an art student, and that she had studied in Paris and Antwerp, had exhibited in Munich and Turin, and was contemplating visiting London the following spring. They talked on in this strain until Hellen, remembering their mission, exclaimed:—

"We must be very close to where I left Schiller. I will call to him."

He did so—not once, but many times; and the reverberation of his voice rang out loud and clear in the silence of the vast, moon-kissed forest. But there was no response, nothing but the rustling of branches and the shivering of leaves.

"What's that?" Marguerite suddenly cried, clutching hold of Hellen's arm. "There! right in front of us, lying on the ground. There!" and she indicated the object with her gleaming finger-tip.

"It looks remarkably like Schiller," Hellen said. "Can he be asleep?"

Quickening their pace, they speedily arrived at the spot. It was Schiller, or rather what had once been Schiller, for there was now very little left of him but the face and hands and feet; the rest had only too obviously been eaten. The spectacle was so shocking that for some minutes Hellen was too overcome to speak.

"It must have been wolves!" he said at length. "I fancied I heard them several times. Would to God I had never left him! What a death!"

"Horrible!" Marguerite whispered, and she turned her head away to avoid so harrowing a sight.

"Well," Hellen observed in a voice broken with emotion, "it's no use staying here. We can't be of any service to him now. I will gather the remains together in the morning, and with the assistance of your father see that they are decently interred. Come! let us be going." And offering Marguerite his arm, they began to retrace their steps.

For some time Hellen was too occupied with thoughts of his friend's cruel death to think of anything else, but the close proximity of Marguerite gradually made itself felt, and by the time they had reached the open clearing—the spot where he had encountered Wilfred—his passion completely overpowered him. Throwing discretion to the winds, and oblivious of wife, children, home, honour, everything save Marguerite—the lustre of her eyes and the dainty curving of her lips—he slipped his arm round her waist, and pressing her close to him, smothered her in kisses.

"How dare you, sir!" she panted, slowly shaking herself free. "Aren't you ashamed of such behaviour? What would your wife say, if she knew?"

"I couldn't help it," Hellen pleaded. "I'm not myself to-night. Your beauty has bewitched me, and I would risk anything to have you in my arms." He spoke so earnestly and looked at her so appealingly that she smiled.

"I know I am beautiful," she said, and the intonation of her voice thrilled him to the very marrow of his bones. "Dozens of men have told me so. Consequently, since there seems to have been some excuse for you, I forgive you, only——," but before she could say another word, Hellen had again seized her, and this time he did not loosen his hold till from sheer exhaustion he could kiss her no more.

"It's no use!" he panted. "I can't help it. I love you as I never loved a woman before, and if you were to ask me to do so I would go to Hell with you this very minute."

"It is dangerous to express such sentiments here," Marguerite said. "Don't you know this spot is full of supernatural influences, and that the first two things you wish for will be granted?"

"I have already wished," Hellen said. "I wished when I was here with your father."

"Then wish again," Marguerite replied; "I assure you your wishes will be fulfilled." And again she looked at him in a way that sent all the blood in his body surging wildly to his head, and roused his passion in hot and furious rebellion against his reason.

"I wish, then," he cried, seizing hold of her hands and pressing them to his lips—"I wish every obstacle removed that prevents my having you always with me—that is wish number one."

"And wish number two?" the girl interrogated, her warm, scented breath fanning his cheeks and nostrils. "Won't you wish that you may be mine for ever? Always mine, mine to eternity!"

"I will!" Hellen cried. "May I be yours always—yours to do what you like with—in this life and the next."

"And now you shall have your reward," Marguerite exclaimed, clapping her hands gleefully. "I will kiss you of my own free will," and throwing her arms round his neck, she drew his head down to hers, and kissed him, kissed him not once but many times.

An hour later they left the spot and slowly made their way to the cottage. As they neared it, loud screams for help rent the air, and Hellen, to his horror, heard his wife and children—he could recognize their individual voices—shrieking to him to save them.

In an instant he was himself again. All his old affection for home and family was restored, and with a loud answering shout he started to rush to their assistance. But Marguerite willed otherwise. With a dexterous movement of her feet she got in his way and tripped him, and before he had time to realize what was happening, she had flung herself on the top of him and pinioned him down.

"No!" she said playfully, "you shall not go! You are mine, mine always, remember, and if I choose to keep you here with me, here you must remain."

He strove to push her off, but he strove in vain; for the slender, rounded limbs he had admired so much possessed sinews of steel, and he was speedily reduced to a state of utter impotence.

The shrieks from the cottage were gradually lapsing into groans and gurgles, all horribly suggestive of what was taking place, but it was not until every sound had ceased that Marguerite permitted Hellen to rise.

"You may go now," she said with a mischievous smile, kissing him gaily on the forehead and giving his cheeks a gentle slap. "Go—and see what a lucky man you are, and how speedily your first wish has been gratified."

Sick with apprehension, Hellen flew to the cottage. His worst forebodings were realized. Stretched on the floor of their respective rooms, with big, gaping wounds in their chests and throats, lay his wife and children; whilst cross-legged, on a chest in the kitchen, his dark saturnine face suffused with glee, squatted Wilfred.

"Fiend!" shouted Hellen. "I understand it all now. I have been dealing with the Spirits of the Harz Mountains. But be you the Devil himself you shan't escape me," and snatching an axe from the wall, he aimed a terrific blow at Wilfred's head.

The weapon passed right through the form of Wilfred, and Hellen, losing his balance, fell heavily to the ground. At this moment Marguerite entered.

"Fool!" she cried; "fool, to think any weapon can harm either Wilfred or me. We are phantasms—phantasms beyond the power of either Heaven or Hell. Come here!"

Impelled by a force he could not resist, Hellen obeyed—and as he gazed into her eyes all his blind infatuation for her came back.

"We must part now," she said; "but only for a while—for remember, you belong to me. Here is a token"—and she thrust into his hand a wisp of her long, golden hair. "Sleep on it and dream of me. Do not look so sad. I shall come for you without fail, and by this sign you shall know when I am coming. When this mark begins to heal," she said, as, with the nail on the forefinger of the right hand, she scratched his forehead, "get ready!"

There was then a loud crash—the room and everything in it swam before Hellen's eyes, the floor rose and fell, and sinking backwards he remembered no more.

When he recovered he was lying in the centre of the haunted plot. There was nothing to be seen around him except the trees—dark lofty pines that, swaying to and fro in the chill night breeze, shook their sombre heads at him. A great sigh of relief broke from him—his experiences of course had only been a dream. He was trying to collect his thoughts, when he discovered that he was holding something tightly clasped in one of his hands. Unable to think what it could be, he rose, and held it in the full light of the moon. He then saw that it was a tuft of white fur—the fur of some animal. Much puzzled, he put it in his pocket, and suddenly recollecting his friend, set out for the place where he had left him. "I shall soon know," he said to himself, "whether I have been asleep all this time—God grant it may be so!" His heart beat fearfully as he pressed forward, and he shouted out "Schiller" several times. But there was no reply, and presently he came upon the remains, just as he had seen them when accompanied by Marguerite. Convinced now that all that had taken place was grim reality, he went back along the route Schiller and he had taken the preceding day, and in due time reached the village. To the landlord of the inn where they had stayed he related what had happened. "I am truly sorry for you," the landlord said; "your experience has indeed been a terrible one. Every one here knows the forest is haunted in that particular spot, and we all give it as wide a berth as possible. But you have been most unfortunate, for Wilfred and Marguerite, who are werwolves, only visit these parts periodically. I last heard of them being seen when I was about ten years of age, and they then ate a pedlar called Schwann and his wife."

As soon as Schiller's remains had been brought to the village and interred in the cemetery, Hellen, armed to the teeth and accompanied by several of the biggest and strongest hounds he could hire—for he could get none of the villagers to go with him—spent a whole day searching for Wilfred's cottage. But although he was convinced he had found the exact spot where it had stood, there were now no traces of it to be seen.

At length he returned to the village, and on the following morning set out for Frankfort. On his arrival home he was immediately apprised of the fact that a terrible tragedy had occurred in his house. His wife and children had been found dead in their beds, with their throats cut and dreadful wounds in their chests, and the police had not been able to find the slightest clue to the murderers. With a terrible sinking at the heart Hellen asked for particulars, and learned, as he knew only too well he would learn, that the date of the tragedy was identical with that of his adventure in the forest.

He tried hard to persuade himself that the coincidence was a mere coincidence; but—he knew better. Besides, there was the scratch!—the scratch on his forehead.

Moreover, the scratch remained. It remained fresh and raw till a few days prior to his death, when it began to heal. And on the day he died it had completely healed.

CHAPTER X

# A Lycanthropous Brook in the Harz Mountains; or, the Case of the Countess Hilda von Breber

ANOTHER CASE OF lycanthropy in Germany, connected with the Harz Mountains, occurred somewhere about the beginning of the last century.

Count Von Breber, chief of the police of Magdeburg, whilst away from home on a holiday with his young and beautiful wife, the Countess Hilda, happened to pass a night in the village of Grautz, in the centre of the Harz Mountains.

In the course of a conversation with the innkeeper, the Countess remarked: "On our way here this morning we crossed a brook, and experienced the greatest difficulty in persuading our dogs to go into the water. It is most unusual, as they are generally only too ready for a dip. Can you in any way account for it?"

"Were there two very tall poplars, one on either side of the brook?" the innkeeper asked; "and did you notice a peculiar—one cannot describe it as altogether unpleasant—smell there?"

"We did!" the Count and Countess exclaimed in chorus.

"Then it was the spot locally known as Wolf Hollow," the innkeeper said. "No one ventures there after dark, as it has a very evil reputation."

"Stuff and nonsense!" the Count snapped.

"That is as your honour pleases," the innkeeper said humbly. "We village folk believe it to be haunted; but, of course, if the subject appears ridiculous to you, I will take care I do not refer to it again."

"Please do!" the Countess cried. "I love anything to do with the supernatural. Tell us all about it."

The innkeeper gave a little nervous cough, and glancing uneasily at the Count, whose face looked more than usually stern in the fading sunlight, observed: "They do say, madam, that whoever drinks the water of that stream——"

"Yes, yes?" the Countess cried eagerly.

"Suffers a grave misfortune."

"Of what nature?" the Countess demanded; but before the innkeeper could answer, the Count cut in:—

"I forbid you to say another word. The Countess has drunk the water there, and your cock-and-bull stories will frighten her into fits. Confess it is all made up for the benefit of travellers like ourselves."

"Yes, your honour!" the innkeeper stammered, his knees shaking; "I confess it is mere talk, but we all be—be—lieve it."

"That will do—go!" the Count cried; and the innkeeper, terrified out of his wits, flew out of the room.

Some minutes later mine host received a peremptory summons to appear before the Count, who was alone and scowling horribly, in the best parlour. He had barely got inside the room before the Count burst out wrathfully:—

"I've sent for you, sir, in order to impress upon you the fact that if either you or your minions mention one word about that brook to the Countess, or to her servants—mark that—I will have the breath flogged out of your body and your tongue snipped. Do you hear?"

"Y—yes, your honour," the innkeeper cried. "I ful—fully un—understand, and if her ladyship asks me any—anything abou—out the br—br—brook, I will lie."

"Which won't trouble you much, eh?"

"N—n—o, your honour! I mean y—yes, your honour! It will be a burden on my con—conscience, but I will do anything to pl—please your honour."

The interview then terminated, and the innkeeper, bathed in perspiration and wishing his lot in life anything but what it was, hastened to prepare dinner.

"I hope nothing dreadful will happen to me; I feel that something will," the Countess said, as she let down her long beautiful hair that night. "Carl, why did you let me drink the water?"

"The water be ——!" the Count growled. "Didn't you hear what the innkeeper said?—that the story was mere invention! If you believe all the idle tales you hear, you will soon be in an asylum. Hilda, I'm ashamed of you!"

"And I'm ashamed of myself," the Countess cried, "so there!" and she flung her arms round his neck and kissed him.

The following morning they left the inn, and, retracing their steps, journeyed homewards. The Count looked at his wife somewhat critically; she was very pale, and there were dark rims under her eyes.

"I do believe, Hilda," he observed with an assumed gaiety, "you are still worrying about that water!"

"I am," she replied; "I had such queer dreams."

He asked her to narrate them, but she refused; and as her sleep now became constantly disturbed, and she was getting thin and worried, the Count determined that as soon as he reached home he would call in a doctor. The latter, examining the Countess, attributed the cause of her indisposition to dyspepsia, and ordered her a diet of milk food. But she did not get better, and now insisted upon sleeping alone, choosing a bedroom situated in a secluded part of the house, where there was absolute silence.

The Count remonstrated. "You might at least let me occupy the room next to you!" he said.

"No," she replied; "I should hear you if you did. I am sensible now of the very slightest sounds, and besides disturbing me, they are a source of the greatest annoyance. I feel I shall never get well again unless I can have complete rest and quiet. Do let me!" and she fixed her big blue eyes on him so earnestly, that he vowed he would see that all her wishes, no matter how fanciful, were gratified.

"I hope she won't go mad!" he said to himself; "her behaviour is odd, to say the least of it. Odd!—wholly inexplicable."

It was rather too bad that just now, when his mind was harassed with misgivings at home, he should also be bothered with disturbances outside his own home. But so it was. Events of an unprecedented nature were taking place in the town, and it fell to his lot to cope with them. Night after night children—mostly of the poorer class—disappeared, and despite frantic yet careful and thorough searches, no clue as to what had befallen them had, so far, been discovered. The Count doubled the men on night duty, but in spite of these and other extraordinary precautions the disappearances continued, and the affair—already of the utmost gravity—promised to be one that would prove disastrous, not merely to the heads of families, but to the head of the police himself. So long as the missing ones had been of the lower orders only, the Count had not had much to fear—the murmurings of their parents could easily be held in check—but now that a few of the children of the rich had been spirited away, there was every likelihood of the matter reaching the ears of the Court. One evening, when the Count had hardly recovered his equanimity after a stormy interview with Herr Meichen, the banker, whose three-year-old daughter had vanished, and a still more distressing scene with Otto Schmidt, the lawyer, whose six-year-old daughter had disappeared, his patience was called upon to undergo a still further trial in consequence of a visit from General Carl Rittenberg, a person of the greatest importance, not only in the town, but in the whole province. Purple in the face with suppressed fury, the General burst into the room where the head of the police sat.

"Count!" he cried, striking the table with his fist, "this is beyond a joke. My child—my only child—Elizabeth, whom my wife and I passionately love, has been stolen. She was walking by my side in Frederick Street this afternoon, and as it suddenly became foggy, I left her a moment to hail a vehicle to take us home. I wasn't gone from her more than half a minute at the most, but when I returned she had gone. I searched everywhere, shouting her name; and passers by, compassionate strangers, joined me in my search; but though we have looked high and low not a trace of her have we been able to discover. I have not told her mother yet. God help me—I dare not! I dare not even show my face at home without her—my wife will never forgive me——"; and so great was his emotion that he buried his face in his hands, and his great body heaved and shook. Then he started to his feet, his eyes bulging and lurid. "Curse you!" he shrieked; "curse you, Count! it's all your fault! Day after day you've sat here, when you ought to have been hunting up these rascally police of yours. You've no right to rest one second—not one second, do you hear?—till the mystery surrounding these poor lost children has been cleared up, and, living or dead—God forbid it should prove to be the latter!—they are restored to their parents. Now, mark my words, Count, unless my child Elizabeth is found, I'll make your name a byword throughout the length and breadth of the country—I'll——"; but words failed him, and, shaking his fist, he staggered out of the room.

The Count was much perturbed. The General was one of the few people in the town who really had it in their power to do him harm—the one man above all others with whom he had hitherto made it his business to keep in. He had not the least doubt but that the General meant all he said, and he recognized only too well that his one and only hope of salvation lay in the recovery of Elizabeth. But, God in heaven, where could he look for her? Sick at heart, he marshalled every policeman in the force, and within an hour every street in Magdeburg was being subjected to a most rigorous search. The Count was just quitting his office, resolved to join in the hunt himself, when a shabbily dressed woman brushed past the custodian at the door, and racing up to him, flung herself at his feet.

"What the devil does she want?" the Count demanded savagely. “Who is she?”

“Martha Brochel, your honour, a poor half-witted creature, who was one of the first in the town to lose a child,” the door-porter replied; “and the shock of it has driven her mad!”

“Mad! mad! Yes! that is just what I am—mad!” the woman broke out. “Everything is in darkness. It is always night! There are no houses, no chimneys, no lanterns, only trees—big, black trees that rustle in the wind, and shake their heads mockingly. And then something hideous comes! What is it? Take it away! Take it away! Give her back to me!” And as Martha’s voice rose to a shriek, she threw her hands over her head, and, clenching them, growled and snarled like a wild animal.

“Put her outside!” the Count said with an impatient gesture; “and take good care she does not get in here again.”

“No! Don’t turn me away! Don’t! don’t!” Martha screamed; “I forgot what it was I wanted to tell you—but I remember now. I’ve seen it!—seen the thing that stole my child. There is light—light again! Oh! hear me!”

“Where have you seen it, Martha?” the porter inquired; and looking at the Count, he said respectfully: “It is just possible, your honour, this woman might be of use to us, and that she has actually seen the person who stole her child.”

“Rubbish! What right has she to have children?” the Count snapped, and he spurned the supplicant with his boot.

The moment she was in the street, however, the head of the police was after her. Keeping close behind her, he resolutely dogged her steps. The evening was now far advanced, and the fog so dense that the Count, though he knew the city, was soon at a total loss as to his whereabouts. But on and on the woman went, now deviating to the right, now to the left; sometimes pausing as if listening, then tearing on again at such a rate that the Count was obliged to run to keep up with her. Suddenly she uttered a shrill cry:

"There it is! There it is! The thing that took my child!" and the figure of what certainly appeared to be a woman, muffled, and carrying a sack on her shoulder, glided across the road just in front of them and disappeared in the impenetrable darkness. Martha sped after her, and the Count, his hopes raised high, followed in hot pursuit. He failed to recognize the ground they were traversing, and presently they came to a high wall, over which Martha scrambled with the agility of an acrobat. The Count, in attempting to imitate her, damaged his knee and tore his clothes, but he also landed safely on the other side. Then on they went, Martha with unabated energy, the Count horribly exhausted, and beginning to think of turning back, when they were abruptly brought to a standstill. The walls of some building loomed right ahead of them. The object of their pursuit, again visible, darted through a doorway; whilst Martha, with a loud cry of triumph, sprang in after her; but before the Count could cross the threshold the door was slammed and locked in his face. Then he heard a chorus of the most appalling sounds—sounds so strange and unearthly that his blood turned to ice and his hair rose straight on end. Rushing footsteps mingled with peculiar soft patterings; agonized human screams coupled with the growls and snappings of an animal; a heavy thud; gurgles; and then silence.

The Count's courage revived: he hurled himself against the

door; it gave with a crash, and the next moment he was inside. But what a sight met his eyes! The place, which somehow or the other seemed oddly familiar to him, was a veritable shambles—floor, walls, and furniture were sodden with blood. In every corner were mangled human remains; whilst stretched on the ground, opposite the doorway, lay the body of Martha, her face unrecognizable and her breast and stomach ripped right open. This was terrible enough, but more terrible by far was the author of it all, who, having cast aside wraps, now stood fully revealed in the yellow glow of a lantern. What the Count saw was a monstrosity—a thing with a woman's breast, a woman's hair, golden and curly, but the face and feet were those of a wolf; whilst the hands, white and slender, were armed with long, glittering nails, cruelly sharp and dripping with blood.

To the Count's astonishment the creature did not attack him, but uttering a low plaintive cry, veered round and endeavoured to escape. But escape was the very last thing Van Breber would permit. Whatever the thing was—beast or devil—it had caused him endless trouble, and if allowed to get away now, would go on with its escapades, and so bring about his ruin. No! he must kill it. Kill it even at the risk of his own life. With a shout of wrath he plunged his sword up to its hilt in the thing's back.

It fell to the floor and the Count bent over it curiously. Something was happening—something strange and terrifying; but he could not look—he was forced to shut his eyes. When he opened them he no longer saw the hairy visage of a wolf—he was gazing fondly into the dying eyes of his beautiful and much-loved wife. With a rapidity like lightning, he recognized his surroundings. He was in a long disused summer-house that stood in a remote corner of his own grounds!

"God help me and you, too!" the Countess Hilda whispered, clasping him fondly in her arms. "It was the water!—the water I drank in the Harz Mountains! I have been bewitched——"; and kissing him feverishly on the lips, she sank back—dead.

## CHAPTER XI

# Werwolves in Austria-Hungary and the Balkan Peninsula

### THE CASE OF THE FAMILY OF KLOSKA AND THE LYCANTHROPOUS FLOWER

In the mountainous regions of Austria-Hungary and the Balkan Peninsula are certain flowers credited with the property of converting into werwolves whoever plucks and wears them. Needless to say, these flowers are very rare, but I have heard of their having been found, comparatively recently, both in the Transylvanian Alps and the Balkans. A story *à propos* of one of these discoveries was told me last summer.

Ivan and Olga were the children of Otto and Vera Kloska—the former a storekeeper of Kerovitch, a village on the Roumanian side of the Transylvanian Alps. One morning they were out with their mother, watching her wash clothes in a brook at the back of their house, when, getting tired of their occupation, they wandered into a thicket.

"Let's make a chaplet of flowers," Olga said, plucking a daisy. "You gather the flowers and I'll weave them together."

"It's not much of a game," Ivan grumbled, "but I can't think of anything more exciting just now, so I'll play it. But let's both make wreaths and see which makes the best."

To this Olga agreed, and they were soon busily hunting amidst the grass and undergrowth, and scrambling into all sorts of possible and impossible places.

Presently Ivan heard a scream, followed by a heavy thud, and running in the direction of the noise, narrowly avoided falling into a pit, the sides of which were partly overgrown with weeds and brambles.

"It's all right," Olga shouted; "I'm not hurt. I landed on soft ground. It's not very deep, and there's such a queer flower here—I don't know what it is; I've never seen one like it before."

Ivan's curiosity thus aroused, he carefully examined the sides of the pit, and, selecting the shallowest spot, lowered himself slowly over and then dropped. It was nothing of a distance, seven or eight feet at the most, and he alighted without mishap on a clump of rank, luxuriant grass. "See! here it is," his sister cried, pointing to a large, very vivid white flower, shaped something like a sunflower, but soft and pulpy, and full of a sweet, nauseating odour. "It's too big to put in a wreath, so I'll wear it in my buttonhole."

"Better not," Ivan said, snatching it from her; "I don't like it. It's a nasty-looking thing. I believe it's a sort of fungus."

Olga then began to cry, and as Ivan was desirous of keeping the peace, he gave her back the flower. She was a prepossessing child, with black hair and large dark eyes, pretty teeth and plump, sunburnt cheeks. Nor was she altogether unaware of her attractions, for even at so early an age she had a goodly share of the inordinate vanity common to her sex, and liked nothing better than appearing out-of-doors in a new frock plentifully besprinkled with rosettes and ribbons. The flower, she told herself, would look well on her scarlet bodice, and would be a good set-off to her black hair and olive complexion. All this was, of course, beyond the comprehension of Ivan, who regarded his sister's weakness with the most supreme contempt, and for his own part was never so happy as when sky-larking with other boys and getting into every conceivable kind of mischief. Yet for all that he was in the main sensible, almost beyond his years, and extremely fond, and—though he would not admit it—proud of Olga.

She fixed the flower in her dress, and imitating to the best of her knowledge the carriage of royalty, strutted up and down, saying "Am I not grand? Don't I look nice? Ivan—salute me!"

And Ivan was preparing to salute her in the proper military style, taught him by a great friend of his in the village, a soldier in the carabineers for whom he had an intense admiration, when his jaw suddenly fell and his eyes bulged.

"Whatever is the matter with you?" Olga asked.

"There's nothing the matter with me," Ivan cried, shrinking away from her; "but there is with you. Don't! don't make such faces—they frighten me," and turning round, he ran to the place where he had made his descent and tried to climb up.

Some minutes later the mother of the children, hearing piercing shrieks for help, flew to the pit, and, missing her footing, slipped over the brink, and falling some ten or more feet, broke one of her legs and otherwise bruised herself. For some seconds she was unconscious, and the first sight that met her eyes on coming to was Ivan kneeling on the ground, feebly endeavouring to hold at bay a gaunt grey wolf that had already bitten him about the legs and thigh, and was now trying hard to fix its wicked white fangs into his throat.

"Help me, mother!" Ivan gasped; "I'm getting exhausted. It's Olga."

"Olga!" the mother screamed, making frantic efforts to come to his assistance. "Olga! what do you mean?"

"It's all owing to a flower—a white flower," Ivan panted; "Olga would pluck it, and no sooner had she fixed it on her dress than she turned into a wolf! Quick, quick! I can't hold it off any longer."

Thus adjured the wretched woman made a terrific effort to rise, and failing in this, clenched her teeth, and, lying down, rolled over and over till she arrived at the spot where the struggle was taking place. By this time, however, the wolf had broken through Ivan's guard, and he was now on his back with his right arm in the grip of his ferocious enemy.

The mother had not a knife, but she had a long steel skewer she used for sticking into a tree as a means of fastening one end of her washing line. She wore it hanging to her girdle, and it was quite by a miracle it had not run into her when she fell.

"Take care, mother," Ivan cried, as she raised it ready to strike; "remember, it is Olga."

This indeed was an ugly fact that the woman in her anxiety to save the boy had forgotten. What should she do? To merely wound the animal would be to make it ten times more savage, in which case it would almost inevitably destroy them both. To kill it would mean killing Olga. Which did she love the most, the boy or the girl? Never was a mother placed in such a dilemma. And she had no time to deliberate, not even a second. God help her, she chose. And like ninety-nine out of a hundred mothers would have done, she chose the boy; he—he at all costs must be saved. She struck, struck with all the pent-up energy of despair, and in her blind, mad zeal she struck again.

The first blow, penetrating the werwolf's eye, sank deep into its brain, but the second blow missed—missed, and falling aslant, alighted on the form beneath.

An hour later a villager on his way home, hearing extraordinary sounds of mirth, went to the side of the pit and peeped over.

"Vera Kloska!" he screamed; "Heaven have mercy on us, what have you there?"

"He! he! he!" came the answer. "He! he! he! My children! Don't they look funny? Olga has such a pretty white flower in her buttonhole, and Ivan a red stain on his forehead. They are deaf—they won't reply when I speak to them. See if you can make them hear."

But the villager shook his head. "They'll never hear again in this world, mad soul," he muttered. "You've murdered them."

Besides this white flower there is a yellow one, of the same shape and size as a snapdragon; and a red one, something similar to an ox-eyed daisy, both of which have the power of metamorphosing the plucker and wearer into a werwolf. Both have the same peculiar vividness of colour, the same thick, sticky sap, and the same sickly, faint odour. They are both natives of Austria-Hungary and the Balkan Peninsula, and are occasionally to be met with in damp, marshy places.

Certain flowers (lilies-of-the-valley, marigolds, and azaleas), as also diamonds, are said to attract werwolves, thus proving a source of danger to those who wear them. And *à propos* of this magnetic property of diamonds the following anecdote comes to me from the Tyrol:—

## A WERWOLF IN INNSBRUCK

Madame Mildau was one of the prettiest women in Innsbruck. She had golden hair, large violet eyes, a smile that would melt a Loyola, and diamonds that set every woman's mouth watering. With such inducements to seduction, how could Madame Mildau help delighting in balls and fêtes, and in promenading constantly before the public? She revelled in a universal admiration—she aimed at a monopoly—and she lived wholly and solely to exact homage. To be deprived of any single opportunity of displaying her charms and consequent triumphs would indeed have been a hardship, and to nothing short of a very serious indisposition would Madame Mildau have sacrificed her pleasure.

Now it so happened that three of the most brilliant entertainments of the season fell on the same night, and Madame Mildau, with all the unreason of her sex, desired to attend each one of them.

"I have accepted these three invitations," she informed her husband, "and to these three balls I mean to go. I shall apportion the time equally between them. You forget," she added, "that the success of these entertainments really depends on me. Crowds go only to see me, and I should never forgive myself if I disappointed them."

But her husband, with the perversity characteristic of gout and middle age, combined, no doubt, with a not unnatural modicum of jealousy, maintained that one such fête should be sufficient amusement for one night. She might take her choice of one; he would on no account permit her to attend all three. Much to his surprise and delight Madame Mildau made no scene, but graciously submitted after a few mild protestations. A little later her husband remarked encouragingly:—

"I congratulate you, Julia, on your philosophy and self-restraint. In yielding to my wishes you have pleased me immeasurably, and I should like to show my gratification in some substantial manner. As it is some months since I gave you a present, I have resolved to make you one now. You may choose what you like."

"I have chosen," Madame Mildau replied calmly.

"What, already!" her husband cried. "You sly creature. You have been keeping this up your sleeve. What is it?"

"A diamond tiara," was the cool reply. "The one you said you could not afford last Christmas."

"Mon Dieu!" her husband gasped. "I shall be ruined."

"You will be ruined if you do not give it to me," Madame Mildau replied, "for in that case I should leave you. I couldn't live with a liar."

Her husband wrung his hands. He implored her to choose something else, but it was of no avail, and within two hours Madame Mildau had visited the jeweller and the tiara was hers.

The eventful day came at last, and Madame Mildau, escorted

by her husband, attended one of the most popular balls of the season. She did not wear her tiara. There had been several highway jewellery robberies in the neighbourhood of late, and she pleased her husband immensely by leaving her diamonds carefully locked up at home.

"You are prudence itself," he said, gazing at her in admiration. "And as a reward you shall dance all the evening whilst I look on and admire you."

But soon Madame Mildau could dance no longer. She had a very bad headache, and begged her husband to take her home. M. Mildau was very sympathetic. He was very sorry for his wife, and suggested that she should take some brandy. She readily agreed that a little brandy might do her good, and they took some together in their bedroom, after which madame's husband remembered little more. He had a vague notion that his wife was rolling his neck-handkerchief round his forehead in the form of a Turkish turban, and patting him on the cheeks and smilingly wishing him a thousand pleasant dreams, and then—all was a blank. He might as well have been dead. With madame it was otherwise. The headache was, of course, a ruse. The brandy she had given her husband had been well drugged, and no sooner had she made sure it had taken effect than she snapped her daintily manicured finger-tips in the air, and retiring to her dressing-room, changed the dress she was wearing for one ten times more costly and beautiful—a dress of rose-coloured gauze, upon which a drapery of lace was suspended by agraffes of diamonds. A wreath of pale roses, that seemed to have been bathed in the dew of the morning, the better to harmonize with the delicate complexion of her lovely face, nestled in her hair, and above it, more magnificent than anything yet seen in Innsbruck, and setting off to perfection the dazzling lustre of her yellow curls, the tiara of diamonds.

After a final survey of herself in the glass, she slipped on her cloak, and stole softly out to join her intimate friend, the Countess Linitz, who was also going to the ball. All things so far had worked wonderfully well; not even a servant suspected her. In order to avoid trusting her secret to anyone in the house, she had employed a stranger to hire an elegant carriage, which was in waiting for her at a discreet distance from the front door. The ball at which Madame Mildau soon arrived with her friend was much more to her liking than the one to which she had been previously escorted by her husband. The music was more harmonious, the conversation more amiable, the dresses more elaborate, and, what was more important than all, Madame Mildau's success was even more instantaneous and complete. The whole room—host, guests, musicians, even waiters—one and all were literally dumbfounded at the extraordinary beauty of her face and costume, to say nothing of her jewels. Such an entrancing spectacle was without parallel in a ballroom in Innsbruck; and when she left, before the entertainment was over, all the life, the light, the gaiety went with her.

But it was at the third ball, to which the same equipage surreptitiously bore her, that Madame Mildau's enjoyment and triumphs reached their zenith; and it was only towards the close of that entertainment—when she felt, by that revelation of instinct which never deceives women on similar occasions, that it was time to depart; that the brilliancy of her eyes, no less than the beauty of her dress, was fading; that her lips, parched with fatigue, had lost that humid red which rendered them so pretty and inviting, and that the dust had taken the beautiful gloss off her hair—that she experienced, for the first time, a sentiment of uneasiness in reviewing the rashness of her conduct. How was it possible, she asked herself, to prevent a casual acquaintance—her friends she could warn—letting out in conversation before her husband that she had been to these balls. And supposing he thus got to know of her deceit, what then?

This idea—the idea of being found out—with all its consequences, rose before her. Her exhausted imagination could find nothing to oppose it, nothing to relieve the feeling of depression which took possession of her, and she almost felt remorse when she threw herself into her carriage. It was a very dark night, cold and windy, and she was only too thankful to nestle close into the soft cushions at her back, and bury her face in the warm fur of her costly wrap. For some minutes she remained absorbed in thought; but it was not long before the monotonous rumble, rumble of the carriage produced a sensation of drowsiness, from which she was rudely awakened by the sound of a cough. Glancing in the direction from whence it came, to her utmost dismay and astonishment she saw, seated in the opposite corner of the vehicle, a young man of good, if somewhat peculiar appearance, and extremely well dressed. Madame Mildau instantly took in all the disadvantages of her situation, and, overwhelmed by the imprudence of her conduct, exclaimed in a tone in which dignity and terror struggled for mastery, "Sir, what audacity!"

"Yes, indeed, what audacity!" the stranger replied, affecting to be shocked. "What pride! What a love of display!" and he rolled his big eyes at her and bared his teeth.

"But, sir," Madame Mildau cried in horror, concluding that the unknown was a madman, "this is *my* carriage. I beg you will depart—I beseech you—I command you. I will summon my servants."

"That will be a vain waste of valuable breath," replied the young man coolly. "You may call your servants—but there is only one, and he is mine. He will not answer you."

"Where am I, then? How infamous!" exclaimed Madame Mildau, and she burst into tears. "Oh, how cruelly punished I am!"

"It is true, madame, you will be punished for having been agreeable, gay, and brilliant to-night without the consent of your husband; but at present he knows nothing about it, for at this moment he reposes in the sleep of the just, confident that you are enjoying the same repose close to him. As to yourself, madame, why this fear? You will have nothing to dread, I assure you, from my indiscretion; but, as you may be aware, there is no fault, however small, that has not its expiation. Nay, do not weep. Am I so ugly? Why should you dread me so, madame? I am a great admirer of your charms, desirous to know you better. Nay, have no suspicions as to my morality—I am no profligate. I came to the ball to-night for quite another purpose."

"Sir, I understand you. You are employed by my husband. A spy! Detestable!"

"Stop, madame," the stranger said, laying his hand gently on hers. "Debase not the dignity of man by imagining for one instant that there is anyone who would lend himself so readily to act the odious part you impute to me. I am no spy."

"In Heaven's name, then," Madame Mildau exclaimed, "what

brings you here? What do you want? Who are you?"

"One at a time, madame," the young man ejaculated. "To begin with, it was those diamonds of yours—those rings on your soft and delicate fingers, those bracelets on your slender rounded wrists, that necklace and pendant on your snowy breast, and over and above all that splendid tiara on your matchless hair. It was the sight of all those bright and gleaming stars that attracted me, just as the light of a candle attracts a moth. I could not resist them."

"Then you—you are a robber!" stammered the lady, ready to faint with terror.

"Wrong again!" the young man said; "I admire your jewels, it is true, but I am no thief."

"Then, in mercy's name, what are you?" demanded the lady.

"Well!" the stranger replied, speaking with a slight snarl, "I am a man now, but I shall soon change."

"A man and will soon change?" Madame Mildau cried; "oh, you're mad, mad—and I'm shut up in here with a lunatic! Help! help!"

"Calmly, calmly," the stranger exclaimed, lifting her hands to his lips and kissing them. "I'm perfectly sane, and at present perfectly harmless. Now tell me, madame—and mind, be candid with me—why don't you love your husband?"

"How do you know I don't?" Madame Mildau faltered.

"Tut, tut!" the young man said. "Anyone could see that with half an eye. Besides, consider your conduct to-night! Answer my questions."

"Well, you see!" Madame Mildau stammered, having come to the conclusion that even if the man were not mad it would be highly impolitic to provoke him, "I'm so much younger than he is. I'm only twenty-three, whereas he is forty-five. Besides, he detests all amusements, and I love them—especially dances. He is too fat to——"

"Are you sure he is fat? Will you swear he is fat?" the stranger asked, grasping her hands so tightly that she screamed.

"I swear it!" she said, "he is quite the fattest man I know."

"And tender! But no, he can't be very tender!"

"What questions to ask!" Madame Mildau said. "How do I know whether he is tender! Besides, what does it concern you?"

"It concerns me much," the young man retorted; "and you, too, madame. You asked me just now a question concerning myself. Your curiosity shall be satisfied. I am a werwolf. My servant on the box who took the place of your employé is a werwolf. In an hour the metamorphosis will take place. You are out here in the Wood of Arlan alone with us."

"In the Wood of Arlan!"

"Yes, madame, in the Wood of Arlan, which is, as you know, one of the wildest and least frequented spots in this part of the Tyrol. We are both ravenously hungry, and—well, you can judge the rest!"

Madame Mildau, who regarded werwolves in the same category as satyrs and mermaids, was once more convinced that she had to deal with a lunatic, but thinking it wisest to humour him, she said, "I shouldn't advise you to eat me. I'm not at all nice. I'm dreadfully tough."

"You're not that," the young man said, "but I'm not at all sure that the paint and powder on your cheeks might not prove injurious. Anyhow, I have decided to spare you on one condition!"

"Yes! and that is?" Madame Mildau exclaimed, clapping her hands joyfully.

"That you let me have your husband instead. Give me the keys of your house, and my man and I will fetch him. Did you leave him sound asleep?"

"Yes!" Madame Mildau faltered.

"In other words you drugged him! I knew it! I can read it in your eyes. Well—so much the better. Your foresight has proved quite providential. We will bind you securely and leave you here whilst we are gone, and when we return with your husband you shall be freed, and my man shall drive you home. The key?"

Madame Mildau gave it him. With the aid of his servant—a huge man, well over six feet and with the chest and limbs of a Hercules—the stranger then proceeded to gag and bind Madame Mildau hand and foot, and lifting her gently on to the road, fastened her securely to the trunk of a tree.

"Au revoir!" he exclaimed, kissing her lightly on the forehead. "We shan't be long! These horses go like the wind."

The next moment he was gone. For some seconds Madame Mildau struggled desperately to free herself; then, recognizing the futility of her efforts, resigned herself to her fate. At last she heard the clatter of horses' hoofs and the rumble of wheels, and in a few minutes she was once again free.

"Quick!" the stranger said, leading her by the arm, "there's not a moment to lose. The transmutation has already begun. In a few seconds we shall both be wolves and your fate will be sealed. We've got your husband, and, fortunately for you, he is as you described him, nice and plump. If you want to take a final peep at him, do so at once; it's your last chance."

But Madame Mildau had no such desire. She moved aside as her husband, clad in his pyjamas and still sleeping soundly, was lifted out of the vehicle and placed on the ground, and then, hurriedly brushing past him, was about to enter the carriage, when the young man interposed.

"On the box, madame. We could not find you a coachman—you must drive yourself; and as you value your life, drive like the——"

But madame did not wait for further instructions. Springing lightly on the box, she picked up the reins, and with a crack of the whip the horses were off. A minute later, and the wild howl of wolves, followed by a piercing human scream, rang out in the still morning air.

"That's my husband! I recognize his voice," Madame Mildau sighed. "Ah, well! thank God, the man wasn't a robber. My diamonds are safe."

CHAPTER XII

# The Werwolf in Spain

**WERWOLVES ARE, PERHAPS,** rather less common in Spain than in any other part of Europe. They are there almost entirely confined to the mountainous regions (more particularly to the Sierra de Guadarrama, the Cantabrian, and the Pyrenees), and are usually of the male species. Generally speaking the property of lycanthropy in Spain appears to be hereditary; and, as one would naturally expect in a country so pronouncedly Roman Catholic, to rid the lycanthropist of his unenviable property it is the custom to resort to exorcism. Though they are extremely rare, both flowers and streams possessing the power of transmitting the property of werwolfery are to be found in the Cantabrian mountains and the Pyrenees.

And in Spain, as in Austria-Hungary, precious stones—particularly rubies—not infrequently, and often with disastrous results, attract the werwolf. The following case of a Spanish werwolf may be taken as typical:—

In the month of September, 1853, a young man, one Paul Nicholas, arrived from Paris at Pamplona, and took up his abode at l'Hôtel Hervada.

He was rich, idle, sleek; and the sole object of his stay at Pamplona was the pursuit of some little adventure wherewith he might be temporarily employed, and whereof perchance he might afterwards boast. Well, in the hotel there had arrived, a day or two before Monsieur Nicholas, a young and beautiful lady, the effect of whose personal attractions was intensified by certain mysterious circumstances. No one knew her; she had no one with her—not even a servant to be bribed—and although eminently fitted to shine in society, she went neither to the opera nor the dance. As may be readily understood, she was soon the sole topic of conversation in the hotel. Every one talked of her rare beauty, elegance, and musical genius, and immediately after dinner, when she retired to her room, many of the guests would steal upstairs after her, and, stationing themselves outside her door, would remain there for hours to listen to her singing.

Paul Nicholas's head was completely turned. To have such a neighbour, with the face and voice of an angel, and yet not to know her! It was enough to drive him wild. At last, to every one's surprise, the mysterious lady, apparently so exclusive, permitted the advances of a very commonplace, middle-aged gentleman with hardly a hair on his head and a paunch that was voted quite disgusting.

The friendship between the two ripened fast. In defiance of all conventionality, the lady took to sitting out late at night with her elderly admirer, and, with an absolute disregard of decorum, accompanied him on long excursions. Finally, she went away with him altogether. On the occasion of this latter event every one in the hotel heaved a sigh of relief, saving Paul.

Paul was disconsolate. He stayed on, hovering about the places she had most frequented, and hoping to see in every fresh arrival at the hotel his adored one come back. His pitiable condition gained no sympathy.

"Silly fellow!" was the general comment. "He is desperately in love! And with such a creature! What an idiot!"

But Paul's patience was at length rewarded, his devotion apparently justified, for the lady returned, unaccompanied; and so great was the charm of her personality that within two days of her reappearance she had completely won back the hearts of her fellow-guests. Again every one raved of her.

Meanwhile, Paul Nicholas became more enamoured than ever. He bought a guitar, and composed love lyrics—which he sang outside her door, from morning till night, with all that wealth of tenderness so uniquely expressible in a human voice—but it was all in vain. For the lady, whose name had at last leaked out—it was Isabelle de Nurrez—had yielded to the attentions of another stout, middle-aged gentleman, with whom in due course she departed.

This was too much even for her most ardent admirers. Every guest in the hotel protested, and petitioned that she might not be readmitted.

But mine host shook his head with scant apology. "I cannot help it," he said. "The lady pays more for her rooms than all the rest of you put together, so why should I turn her out? After all, if she likes to have many sweethearts, why shouldn't she? It is her own concern, neither yours nor mine. It harms no one!"

And some of the guests, seeing logic in their landlord's views, remained; others went. As for Paul, he was immeasurably shocked at the bad taste of his adored one; but he stayed on, and within a few days, as he had fondly hoped, the fickle creature returned—and, as before, returned alone. It was then that he resolved on writing to her. With a crow-quill almost as fine as the long silky eyelashes of Isabella, on a sheet of paper whose border of Cupids, grapes, vases, and roses left little—too little—space for writing, he indited his letter, which, when completed, he sealed with a seal of azure blue wax, bearing the device of a dove ready for flight. And so scented was this epistle that it perfumed the entire hotel in its transit by means of a servant (well paid for the purpose) to mademoiselle's room. Again—this time for an endless amount of trouble and expense—Paul was rewarded. When next he met mademoiselle, and an opportune moment arrived, she looked at him, and as her lovely eyes scanned his manly, if somewhat portly figure, she smiled—smiled a smile of satisfaction which meant much. Paul Nicholas was in ecstasies. He hardly knew how to contain himself; he sighed, radiated, and wriggled about to such an extent that the attention of every one in the place was directed to him; whereupon Mlle de Nurrez turned very red and frowned. Paul's expectations now sank to zero; for the rest of the day he was almost too miserable to live. But Mlle de Nurrez, no doubt perceiving him to be truly penitent for having so embarrassed her, forgave him, and on his way to dinner he received a note in her own pretty handwriting giving him permission to make her acquaintance without any further introduction. The way thus paved, Monsieur Paul Nicholas, overjoyed, lost no time in seeking out the lady. She was singing a wild sweet song as he entered her sitting-room, and her back, turned to the door, gave him an opportunity of observing, as she leant over her guitar, the most exquisite shoulders and the prettiest-shaped head in the world. With graceful confusion she rose to greet him, and her long eyelashes fell over eyes black and brilliant as those that awakened the furore of two continents—the eyes of Lola Montez. She was dressed in white; her rich dark hair was held in place with combs of gold; her girdle was of gold, and so also were the massive bracelets on her arms, which—so perfect was their symmetry—might well have been fashioned by a sculptor.

Monsieur Paul Nicholas, with the air of a prince, escorted her to the dining-room; and over champagne, coffee, and liqueurs their friendship grew apace. Some hours later, when ensconced together in a cosy retreat on the terrace, and the fast disappearing lights in the hotel windows warned them it would soon be prudent to retire, Mlle de Nurrez exclaimed with a sigh:—

"You have told me so much about yourself, whilst I—I have told you nothing in return. Alas! I have a history. My parents are dead—my mother died when I was a baby, and my father, who was a very wealthy man—having accumulated his money in the business of a cork merchant which he carried on for years in Portugal—died just six months ago. He was on a voyage for his health in the Mediterranean, when he formed an acquaintance with a young Hindu, Prince Dajarah who soon acquired unbounded influence over him. My father died on this voyage, and—God forgive my suspicions!—but his death was strange and sudden. On opening his will, it was found that all his property was left to me—but only on the condition that

I married Prince Dajarah."

"Marry a black man! Mon Dieu, how terrible!" Paul Nicholas cried.

"You are right. It was terrible!" Mlle de Nurrez went on. "And if I refused to marry Prince Dajarah, he, according to the will, would inherit everything. Well, Prince Dajarah was persistent; he declared that it was my duty to marry him, to fulfil my father's dying wish. It was in vain that I implored his mercy—that I told him I could never return his affections. And at last, finding that upon Prince Dajarah neither remonstrance nor reproach had any effect, I fled to a town some ten miles distant from this hotel, taking with me what money and jewellery I possessed.

"Alas! he soon discovered my whereabouts, and with the sole object of continuing his persecution of me, speedily established himself in the house—which, unfortunately for me, happened to be vacant—next to mine. My money is nearly exhausted, I have no resources, and unless some one intervenes, some one brave and fearless, some one who really loves me, I shall undoubtedly be forced into a marriage with this odious wretch. Heavens, the bare idea of it is poisonous! You remember the two men who paid such marked attentions to me a short time ago?"

Paul Nicholas nodded. His emotion was such he could not speak.

"They both imagined they were in love with me. They swore they would confront the black tyrant and kill him; but when they were put to the test—when I took them and pointed him out to them—they went white as a sheet, and—fled."

"Why torture me thus?" Paul Nicholas cried. "Tell me—only tell me what it is you want me to do!"

"Do you love me?"

"More than my life."

"More than your soul?"

"More than my soul."

"Will you save me from a fate more horrible than death?"

"If I go to Hell for you—yes!" Paul said, gazing on a face lovely as a dream.

"You must come with me to his house to-morrow then! You must come armed. You must kill him."

"Kill him!" Paul cried, turning pale.

"Well?"

"But it will be murder—assassination."

"Murder, to kill him—a tyrant—a black man! Bah! Are you too a coward?" And she sprang to her feet, the veins swelling on her white brow, her cheeks colouring, her eyes flashing fire, as if she, at least, knew not the meaning of fear. "Sooner than let such a wretch inherit my father's wealth," she cried out, "I will kill him myself—kill him, or perish in the attempt."

Paul Nicholas encountered the earnest gaze of her large, bright eyes, the pleading of her beautiful mouth, and the sweetness of her breath fanned his nostrils. A terrific wave of passion swept over him. He loved as he had never loved before—as he had never deemed it possible to love: and in his mad worship of the woman he believed to be as pure as she was fair, he forgot that the devil hides safest where he is least suspected. Seizing her small white hands in his, he swore upon them to do her will; and he would have gone on making all sorts of wild, impassioned speeches had not Mlle de Nurrez reminded him that it was past locking-up time.

She crossed the main hall of the hotel with him, and as she turned to bid him good night prior to ascending to her quarters, her eyes met his—met his in one long, lingering glance that he assured himself could only have meant love.

Next morning the guests in the hotel received another shock. Mlle de Nurrez had gone off again—this time with Monsieur Paul Nicholas—that good-looking, well-to-do young man, at whom all the matrons with marriageable daughters had in vain cast longing eyes.

Now, although Paul Nicholas had little knowledge of geography, he could not help remarking, as he journeyed with Mlle Nurrez, that their route was in an exactly opposite direction to that leading to the town which his companion had named to him as her place of residence. He pointed out his difficulty, but Mlle de Nurrez only laughed.

"Wait!" she said. "Wait and see. We shall get there all right. You must trust to my wit."

Paul Nicholas made no further comment. He was already in the seventh heaven—that was enough for him; and leaning back, he continued gazing at her profile.

The afternoon passed away, the sun sank, and night and its shadows moved solemnly on them. Gradually the roadside trees became distinguishable only as deeper masses of shadow, and Paul Nicholas could only tell they were trees by the peculiar sodden odour that, from time to time, sluggishly flowed in at the open window of the carriage. Of necessity, they were proceeding slowly—the road was for the most part uphill, and the horses, though tough and hardy natives of the mountains, had begun to show signs of flagging. They did not pass by a soul, and even the sighs of astonished cattle, whose ruminating slumbers they had routed, at last became events of the greatest rarity. At each yard they advanced the wildness of the country increased, and although the landscape was hidden, its influence was felt. Paul Nicholas knew, as well as if he had seen them, that he was in the presence of grotesque, isolated boulders, wide patches of bare, desolate soil, gaunt trees, and profound straggling fissures.

Being so long confined in a limited space, although in that space was a paradise, he felt the exquisite agony of cramp, and when, after sundry attempts to stretch himself, he at length found a position that afforded him temporary relief, it was only to become aware of a more refined species of torture. The springs of the carriage rising and falling regularly, produced a rhythmical beat, which began to painfully absorb his attention, and to slowly merge into a senseless echo of one of his observations to Mlle de Nurrez. And when he was becoming reconciled to this inferno, another forced itself upon him. How quiet the driver was! Was there any driver? He couldn't see any. Possibly, nay, probably—why not?—the driver was lying gagged and bound on the roadside, and a bandit, one of the notorious Spanish bandits, against whom his friends in Paris had so emphatically warned him, was on the box driving him to his obscure lair in the heart of the mountains. Or was the original driver himself a bandit, and the beautiful girl reclining on the cushions a bandit's daughter? He dozed, and on coming to his waking senses again, discovered that the darkness had slightly lifted. He could see the distant horizon, defined by inky woods, outlined on a lighter sky. A few stars, scattered here and there in this tableau, whilst emphasizing the vastness of the space overhead—a vastness that was positively annihilating—at the same time conveyed a sense of solitude and loneliness, in perfect harmony with the trees, and rocks, and gorges. The effect was only transitory, for with a suddenness almost reminding one of stage mechanism, the moon burst through its temporary covering of clouds, and in a moment the whole country-side was illumined with a soft white glow. It was a warm night, and the breeze that rolled down from the mountain peaks, so remote and passionless, was charged to overflowing with resinous odours, mingled with which, and just strong enough to be recognizable, was the faint, pungent smell of decay. A couple of hares, looking somewhat ashamed of themselves, sprang into upright positions, and with frightened whisks of their tails disappeared into a clump of ferns. With a startled hiss a big snake drew back under cover of a boulder, and a hawk, balked of its prey by the sudden brilliant metamorphosis, uttered an indignant croak. But none of these protests against the moon's innocent behaviour were heeded by Paul Nicholas, whose whole attention was riveted on a large sombre building standing close by the side of the road. At the first glimpse of the place, so huge, grim, and silent, he was seized with a sensation of absolute terror. Nothing mortal could surely inhabit such a house. The dark, frowning walls and vacant, eye-like windows threw back a thousand shadows, and suggested as many eerie fancies—fancies that were corroborated by a few rank sedges and two or three white trunks of decayed trees that rose up on either side of the building; but of life—human life—there was not the barest suspicion.

"What a nightmare of a house!" Paul Nicholas exclaimed, gazing with a shudder upon the remodelled and inverted images of the grey sedge, the ghastly tree-stems, and the vacant, eye-like windows in a black and lurid tarn that lay in unruffled lustre along the edge of the wood.

"It's where he lives!" Mlle de Nurrez whispered.

"What! do you mean to say that it is to this house you have brought me?" Paul shrieked. "To this awful, deserted ghostly mansion! Why have you lied to me?"

"I was afraid you wouldn't care to come if I described the place too accurately," Mlle de Nurrez said. "Forgive me—and pity me, too, for it is here that Prince Dajarah would have me spend my life."

Paul trembled.

"For God's sake, don't desert me!" Mlle de Nurrez exclaimed, laying her hand softly on his shoulder. "Think of the terrible fate that will befall me! Think of your promises, your vows!"

But Paul Nicholas did not respond all at once. His brain was in a whirl. He had been deceived, cruelly deceived! And with what motive? Was Mlle de Nurrez's explanation genuine? Could there be anything genuine about a girl who told an untruth? Once a liar always a liar! Did not that maxim hold good? Was it not one he had heard repeatedly from childhood? What should he do? What could he do? He was here, alone with this woman and her coachman, in one of the wildest and most outlandish regions of Spain. God alone knew where! To attempt to return would be hopeless—sheer imbecility; he would most certainly get lost on the mountains, and perish from hunger and thirst, or fall over some precipice, or into the jaws of a bear; or, at all events, come to some kind of an untimely end. No! there was no alternative, he must remain and trust in Mlle de Nurrez. But the house was appalling; he did not like looking at it, and the bare thought of its interior froze his blood. Then he awoke to the fact that she was still addressing him, that her soft hands were lying on his, that her beautiful eyes were gazing entreatingly at him, that her full ripe lips were within a few inches of his own. The moon lent her its glamour, and his old love reasserting itself with quick, tempestuous force, he drew her into his arms and kissed her repeatedly. Some minutes later and they had crossed the threshold of the mansion. All was as he had pictured it—grim and hushed, and bathed in moonbeams.

The coachman led the way, and with muffled, stealthy footstep conducted them across dark halls and along intricate passages, up long and winding staircases—all bare and cold; through vast gloomy rooms, the walls and floors of which were of black oak, the former richly carved, and in places hung with ancient tapestry, displaying the most grotesque and startling devices. The windows, long, narrow, and pointed, with trellised panes, were at so great a height from the ground that the light was limited, and whilst certain spots were illuminated, many of the remoter angles and recesses were left in total darkness. Monsieur Paul Nicholas did not attempt to explore. At each step he took he fully anticipated a something, too dreadful to imagine, would spring out on him. The rustling of drapery and the rattling of phantasmagoric armorial trophies, in response to the vibration of their footsteps, made his hair stand on end, and he was reduced to a state of the most abject terror long before they arrived at their destination.

At last he was ushered into a small, bare, dimly lighted room. From the centre of the ceiling was suspended an oil lamp, and immediately under it was a marble table. Walls and floor were composed of rough uncovered granite. The atmosphere was fetid, and tainted with the same peculiar, pungent odour noticeable outside.

"This is the room," Mlle de Nurrez said. "Prince Dajarah will be here in a minute. Have you your pistol ready?"

"Yes, see!" and Paul Nicholas pulled it out from his coat-pocket and showed it her.

"Have you any other weapons?" she asked, examining it curiously.

"Yes, a sheath-knife," Paul Nicholas replied a trifle nervously.

"Let me look at it," Mlle de Nurrez exclaimed. "I have a weakness for knives—a rather uncommon trait in a woman, isn't it?"

He handed it to her, and she fingered the blade cautiously. Then with a sudden movement she leaped away from him.

"Fool!" she cried. "Do you think I could ever love a man as fat as you? The story I told you was a lie from beginning to end. I don't remember either of my parents—my mother ran away from home when I was two, and my father died the following year. I married entirely of my own free will—married the man I loved, and he—happened to be a werwolf!"

"A werwolf!" Paul Nicholas shrieked. "God help me! I thought there were no such things!"

"Not in France, perhaps," Mlle de Nurrez said derisively; "but in Spain, in the Pyrenees, many! At certain times of the year my husband won't touch animal food, and if I didn't procure him human flesh he would die of starvation, or in sheer despair eat me. Here he is."

And as she spoke the door opened, and on the threshold stood a singularly handsome young man clad in the gay uniform of a Carlist general.

"Capital!" he exclaimed, as his eyes fell on Paul. "Magnificent! He is quite as fat as the other two. How clever of you, darling!" and throwing his arms round her, he embraced her tenderly. A few seconds later and he suddenly thrust her from him.

"Quick! quick!" he cried. "Run away, darling! run away instantly. I can feel myself changing!" and he pushed her gently to the door.

Mlle de Nurrez took one glance at Paul as she left the room. "Poor fool!" she said, half pityingly, half mockingly. "Poor fat fool! Though you may no longer believe in women you will certainly believe in werwolves—now." And as the door slammed after her, the wildest of shrieks from within demonstrated that, for once in her life, Mlle de Nurrez had spoken the truth.

CHAPTER XIII

# The Werwolf in Belgium and The Netherlands

**BELGIUM ABOUNDS IN** stories of werwolves, all more or less of the same type. As in France, the werwolf, in Belgium, is not restricted to one sex, but is, in an equal proportion, common to both.

By far the greater number of werwolfery cases in this country are to be met with amongst the sand-dunes on the sea coast. They also occur in the district of the Sambre; but I have never heard of any lycanthropous streams or pools in Belgium, nor yet of any wolf-producing flowers, such as are, at times, found in the Balkan Peninsula.

Though the property of lycanthropy here as elsewhere has been acquired through the invocation of spirits—the ceremony being much the same as that described in an earlier chapter—nearly all the cases of werwolfery in Belgium are hereditary.

In Belgium, as in other Roman Catholic countries, great faith is attached to exorcism, and for the expulsion of every sort of "evil spirit" various methods of exorcism are employed. For example, a werwolf is sprinkled with a compound either of 1/2 ounce of sulphur, 4 drachms of asafœtida, 1/4 ounce of castoreum; or of 3/4 ounce of hypericum in 3 ounces of vinegar; or with a solution of carbolic acid further diluted with a pint of clear spring water. The sprinkling must be done over the head and shoulders, and the werwolf must at the same time be addressed in his Christian name. But as to the success or non-success of these various methods of exorcism I cannot make any positive statement. I have neither sufficient evidence to affirm their efficacy nor to deny it. Rye and mistletoe are considered safeguards against werwolves, as is also a sprig from a mountain ash. This latter tree, by the way, attracts evil spirits in some countries—Ireland, India, Spain, for instance—and repels them in others. It was held in high esteem, as a preservative against phantasms and witches, by the Druids, and it may to this day be seen growing, more frequently than any other, in the neighbourhood of Druidical circles, both in Great Britain and on the Continent.

In many parts of Belgium the peasantry would not consider their house safe unless a mountain ash were growing within a few feet of it.

## A CASE OF WERWOLVES IN THE ARDENNES

A case of werwolfery is reported to have happened, not so long ago, in the Ardennes. A young man, named Bernard Vernand, was returning home one night from his work in the fields, when his dog suddenly began to bark savagely, whilst its hair stood on end. The next moment there was a crackle in the hedge by the roadside, and three trampish-looking men slouched out. They looked at Vernand, and, remarking that it was beautiful weather, followed closely at his heels.

Vernand noticed that the eyebrows of all three met in a point over their noses, a peculiarity which gave them a very singular and unpleasant appearance. When he quickened his pace, they quickened theirs; whilst his dog still continued to bark and show every indication of excessive fear. In this way they all four proceeded till they came to a very dark spot in the road, where the trees nearly met overhead. The sound of their footsteps then suddenly ceased, and Vernand, peeping stealthily round, perceived to his horror lurid eyes—that were not the eyes of human beings—glaring after him. His dog took to its heels and fled, and, ignominious though he felt it to be, Vernand followed suit. The next moment there was a chorus of piercing whines, and a loud pattering of heavy feet announced the fact that he was pursued.

Fortunately Vernand was a fast runner—he had carried off many prizes in races at the village fair—and now that he was running for his life, he went like the wind.

But his pursuers were fleet of foot, too, and, despite his pace, they gradually gained on him. Happily for Vernand, he retained a certain amount of presence of mind, and possessing rather more wit than many of the peasants, he suddenly bethought him of a possible avenue of escape. In a conversation with the pastor of the village some months before, the latter had told him how an old woman had once escaped from a wode [5] by climbing up a mountain ash. And if, reasoned Vernand, the ash is a protection against one form of evil spirits, why not against another? He recollected that there was an

5 A phantom horseman, that goes hunting on certain nights in the year, accompanied by phantom dogs. The author has witnessed the phenomenon himself.

ash-tree close at hand, and diverting his course, he instantly headed for it. Not a moment too soon. As he swarmed up the slender trunk, his pursuers—three monstrous werwolves—came to a dead halt at the foot of the tree. However, after giving vent to the disappointment of losing their supper in a series of prodigious howls, they veered round and bounded off, doubtless in pursuit of a less knowing prey.

## A SIMILAR CASE NEAR WATERLOO

A similar case once happened to a young man when returning from Quatre Bras to Waterloo. He was attacked by three werwolves and saved himself by leaping into a rye-field.

## A CASE ON THE SAND-DUNES

The following story of werwolfery is of traditional authenticity only:—

Von Grumboldt, a young man of good appearance, and his sweetheart, Nina Gosset, were out walking together one evening on the sand-dunes near Nina's home, when Von Grumboldt uttered an exclamation of astonishment, and bending down, picked up something which he excitedly showed to Nina. It was a girdle composed of dark, plaited hair fastened with a plain gold buckle. To the young man's surprise Nina shrank away from it.

"Oh!" she cried, "don't touch it! I don't know why—but it gives me such a horrid impression. I'm sure there is an unpleasant history attached to it."

"Pooh!" Von Grumboldt said laughingly; "that's only your fancy. I think it would look remarkably well round your waist," and he made pretence to encircle her with it.

Nina, turning very white, fainted, and Von Grumboldt, who was really very much in love with her, was greatly alarmed. He ran to a brook, fetched some water, and sprinkled her forehead with it. To his intense relief his sweetheart soon came to. As soon as she could speak she implored him, as he valued her life, on no account to touch her with the girdle. To this request Von Grumboldt readily assented, and whistling to his dog—a big collie—in spite of Nina's protests and the animal's frantic struggles, he playfully fastened the belt round the creature's body. Then turning to Nina he began: "Doesn't Nippo (that was the collie's name) look fine——" and suddenly left off. The expression in Nina's eyes made his blood run cold.

"For Heaven's sake," he cried, "what is it? What's the matter?"

White as death again, Nina pointed a finger, and Von Grumboldt, looking in the direction she indicated, saw—not Nippo, but an awful-looking thing in Nippo's place—a big black object, partly dog and partly some other animal, that grew and grew until, within a few seconds, it had grown to at least thrice Nippo's size. With a hideous howl it rushed at Von Grumboldt. The latter, though a strong athletic young man, was speedily overcome, and being dashed to the ground, would soon have been torn to pieces had not Nina, recovering from a temporary helplessness, come to the rescue.

Catching hold of the girdle round the creature's body, she unclasped the buckle, and in a trice the evil thing had vanished; and there was Nippo, his own self, standing before them.

"It is a werwolf belt!" Nina exclaimed, throwing it away from her. "You see, I was right; it is devilish, and no doubt belongs to some one near here who practises Black Magic—Mad Valerie, perhaps. This cross that I wear round my neck, which is made of yew, no doubt warned me of this danger and so saved me from an awful fate. You smile!—but I am certain of it. The yew-tree is just as efficacious in the case of evil spirits as the ash!"

"What shall we do with the beastly thing?" Von Grumboldt asked. "It doesn't seem right to leave it here, in case some one else, with less sense than you, should find it and a dreadful catastrophe result."

"We must burn it," Nina said. "That's the only way of getting rid of the evil influence. Let us do so at once."

Von Grumboldt was nothing loath, and in a few minutes all that remained of the lycanthropous girdle was a tiny heap of ashes.

To burn the object to which the lycanthropous property is attached is the only recognized method of destroying that property. I have had many proofs, too, of the efficacy of burning in the case of superphysical influences other than lycanthropy; such, for example, as haunted furniture, trees, and buildings; and I am quite sure the one and only way to get rid of an occult presence attached to any particular object is to burn that object.

I have been told of "burning" having been successfully practised in the following cases:—

*Case No. 1.*—A barrow in the North of England that had long been haunted by a Barrowian order of Elemental. (The barrow was excavated, and when the remains therein had been burnt, the hauntings ceased.)

*Case No. 2.*—A cave in Wales haunted by the phantasm of a horse, though, whether the real spirit of the horse or merely an Elemental I cannot say. (On the soil in the cave being excavated, and the several skeletons, presumably of prehistoric animals, found being burnt, there were no longer any disturbances.)

*Case No. 3.*—A house in London containing an oak chest, attached to which was the phantasm of an old woman, who used to disturb the inmates of the place nightly. (On the chest being burnt she was seen no more.)

*Case No. 4.*—A tree in Ireland, haunted every night by a Vagrarian. (Immediately after the tree had been burnt the manifestations ceased.)

Burial is a great mistake. As long as a single bone remains, the spirit of the dead person may still be attracted to it, and consequently remain earthbound; but when the corpse is cremated, and the ashes scattered abroad, then the spirit is set free. And, for this reason alone, I advocate cremation as the best method possible of dealing with a corpse.

Before concluding this chapter on the werwolf in Belgium, let me add that werwolfery was not the only form of lycanthropy in that country. According to Grimm, in his "Deutsche Sagen," two warlocks who were executed in the year 1810 at Liége for having, under the form of werwolves, killed and eaten several children, had as their colleague a boy of twelve years of age. The boy, in the form of a raven, consumed those portions of the prey which the warlocks left.

## WERWOLVES IN THE NETHERLANDS

Cases of werwolves are of less frequent occurrence in Holland than in either France or Belgium. Also, they are almost entirely restricted to the male sex.

Exorcism here is seldom practised, the working of a spell being the usual means employed for getting rid of the evil property. The procedure in working the spell is as follows:—

First of all, a night when the moon is in the full is selected. Then at twelve o'clock the werwolf is seized, securely bound, and taken to an isolated spot. Here, a circle of about seven feet in diameter is carefully inscribed on the ground, and in the exact centre of it the werwolf is placed, and so fastened that he cannot possibly get away. Then three girls—always girls—come forward armed with ash twigs with which they flog him most unmercifully, calling out as they do so:—

"Greywolf ugly, greywolf old,
Do at once as you are told.
Leave this man and fly away—
Right away, far away,
Where 'tis night and never day."

They keep on repeating these words and whipping him; and it is not until the face, back, and limbs of the werwolf are covered with blood that they desist.

The oldest person present then comes forward and gives the werwolf a hearty kick, saying as he (or she) does so:—

"Go, fly, away to the sky;
Devil of greywolf, thee we defy.
Out, out, with a howl and yell,'
Twill carry thee faster and surer to hell."

Every one present then dips a cup or mug in a concoction of sulphur, tar, vinegar, and castoreum, just removed from boiling-point, and, forming a circle round the werwolf, they souse him all over with this unpleasant and painfully hot mixture, calling out as they do so:—

"Away, away, shoo, shoo, shoo!
Do you think we care a jot for you?
We'll whip thee again, with a crack, crack, crack!
Scourge thee and beat thee till thou art black;
Fool of a greywolf, we have thee at last,
Back to thy hell home, out of him fast—
Fast, fast, fast!
Our patience won't last.
We'll scratch thee, we'll prick thee,
We'll prod thee, we'll scald thee.
Fast, fast, out of him, fast!"

They keep on shouting these words over and over again till the liquid has given out and the clock strikes one; when, with a final blow or kick at the prostrate werwolf, they run away.

The evil spirit is then said to leave the man, who quickly recovers his proper shape, and with a loud cry of joy rushes after his friends and relations.

When the Spaniards invaded Holland they resorted to a surer, if a somewhat more drastic, mode of getting rid of lycanthropy—they burned the subject possessed of it.

One of the best known cases of a werwolf in the Netherlands is as follows:—

A young man, whilst on his way to a shooting match at Rousse, was suddenly startled by hearing loud screams for help proceeding from a field a few yards distant. To jump a dike and scramble over a low wall was but the work of a few seconds, and in less time than it takes to tell, the young man, whose name was Van Renner, found himself face to face with a huge grey wolf. Quick as thought, he fitted an arrow to his bow, and shot. The missile struck the wolf in the side, and with a howl of pain the wounded creature turned tail and fled for his life.

All might now have ended like some delightful romance, for the rescued one proved to be an exceedingly attractive maiden, with bright yellow hair and big blue eyes; but unfortunately—or perhaps fortunately, who knows?—the girl had a husband, and Van Renner a wife; and so, instead of the incident being the prelude to a love affair, it was merely an occasion for grateful acknowledgment—and—farewell. On his return home that evening Van Renner was met with an urgent request to visit his friend, the Burgomaster. He hastened to obey the summons, and found the Burgomaster in bed, suffering agonies of pain from a wound which he had received in his side some hours previously.

"I can't die without telling you," he whispered, clutching Van Renner by the hand. "God help me, I'm a werwolf! I've always been one. It's in my family—it's hereditary. It was your arrow that has wounded me fatally."

Van Renner was too aghast to speak. He was really fond of the Burgomaster, and to think of him a werwolf—well! it was too dreadful to contemplate. The dying man gazed eagerly, hungrily, piteously into his friend's face.

"Don't say you hate me," he cried. "There is little hope for me, if any, in the next world; and in all probability I shall either go direct to hell or remain earthbound; but, for God's sake, let me die in the knowledge that I leave behind me at least one friend!"

Van Renner tried hard to speak; he made every effort to speak; his lungs swelled, his tongue wobbled, the muscles of his lips twitched; but not a syllable could he utter—and the Burgomaster died.

CHAPTER XIV

# The Werwolves and Maras of Denmark

SINCE SO MUCH has already been written upon the subject of werwolves in Denmark, it is my intention only to touch upon it briefly. It is, I believe, generally acknowledged that, at one time, werwolves were to be met with almost daily in Denmark, and that they were almost always of the male sex; but I can find no records of any particular form of exorcism practised by the Danes with the object of getting rid of the werwolf, nor of any spell used by them for the same purpose; neither does there appear to be, amongst their traditions, any reference to a lycanthropous flower or stream. Opinions differ as to whether werwolves are yet to be found in Denmark, but, from all I have heard, I am inclined to think that they still exist in the more remote districts of that country. The following case may be regarded as illustrative of a typical Danish werwolf:—

## THE CASE OF PETER ANDERSEN, WERWOLF

Peter Andersen, who was a werwolf by descent, his ancestors having been werwolves for countless generations, fell in love with a beautiful young girl named Elisa, and without telling her he was a werwolf, for fear that she would give him up, married her.

Shortly after his marriage, he was returning home one evening with Elisa from a neighbouring fair, where there had been much merrymaking, when, suddenly feeling that the metamorphosis was coming on, he got down from the cart in which they were driving, and said to his wife, very earnestly, "If anything comes towards you, do not be afraid, and do not hurt it; merely strike it with your apron." He then ran off at a great rate into the fields, leaving Elisa very much surprised and impressed. A few minutes afterwards she heard the howl of a wild animal, and, while she was holding in the horse and endeavouring to pacify it, a huge grey wolf suddenly leaped into the road and sprang at her.

Recollecting what her husband had told her, with wonderful presence of mind she whipped off her apron and struck the wolf in the face with it. The animal tore at the apron, and biting a piece out of it, turned tail and ran away. Some time afterwards Andersen returned, and holding out to Elisa the missing piece of her apron, asked if she guessed how he came by it.

"Good God, man!" Elisa cried, the pupils of her eyes dilating with terror, "it was you! I know it by the expression in your face. Heaven preserve me! You're a werwolf!"

"I was a werwolf," Peter said, "but thanks to your brave action in throwing the apron in my face, I am one no longer. I know I did wrong in not telling you of my misfortune before we were married, but I dreaded the idea of losing you. Forgive me, forgive me, I implore you!" and Elisa, after some slight hesitation, granted his request.

This method of getting rid of the lycanthropous spirit seems to have been (and still to be) the one most in vogue in Denmark.

Another well-known story, of a similar kind, is to the effect that while a party of haymakers were at work in a field, a man, who, like Andersen, had kept the fact of his being a werwolf from his family, feeling that he was about to be transmuted, gave his son injunctions that if an animal approached him he was on no account to hurt it, but merely to throw his hat at it. The boy promising to obey, the father hastily left the field. Some minutes later a grey wolf appeared, swimming a stream. It rushed at the boy, who, mad with terror, forgot his father's instructions, and struck at it with a pitchfork.

The prongs of the fork, entering the wolf's side, pierced its heart; and transmutation again taking place, to the horror of all present there lay on the ground, not the body of a beast, but the corpse of the boy's father.

In Denmark it is said that if a woman stretches between four sticks the membrane of a newly born foal, and creeps through it naked, she will bring forth children without pain, but all the boys will be werwolves and the girls maras.

As is the case with the werwolf of other countries, the Danish werwolf retains its human form by day; but after sunset, unlike the werwolf of any other nationality, it sometimes adopts the shape of a dog on three legs before it finally metamorphoses into a wolf.

In addition to these methods (alluded to above) of expelling a lycanthropous spirit in Denmark, there may be added that of addressing the obsessed person as a werwolf and reproaching him roundly. But as I have no proof of the effectiveness of this crude mode of exorcism, I cannot commit myself to any verdict with regard to it.

## MARAS

The mara, to which I have briefly alluded in a foregoing chapter, is to be met with in Denmark almost as often as the werwolf; and the superphysical property, characteristic of the mara no less than of the werwolf, justifies me in a somewhat detailed description of the former here.

A mara is popularly understood to be a woman by day and at night a spirit that torments human beings and horses by sitting astride them and causing them nightmare.

In the main I agree with this definition; though I am inclined to think that the mara is, in reality, less hoydenish and more subtle and complex than public opinion would have us believe. In all probability maras are women who have either inherited or, by the practice of Black Magic, acquired the faculty of a certain species of projection—differing from the projection which is common to both sexes in the following points, viz., that it can always be accomplished (during certain hours) at will; that it is invariably practised with the sole desire to do ill; that the projected spirit is fully conscious of all that is happening around it; and that it possesses most—if not all—of the faculties, motives, and nervous susceptibilities of the physical body.

Whatever may be the character of the mara by day, she is essentially mischievous by night—owing, no doubt, to the fact that this faculty of projection has come to her through the occult powers inimical to man.

From the complexity of their nature, maras present the same difficulty of classification as werwolves—both are human, both are Elemental, and consequently both are an anomaly.

The belief in maras is still prevalent in all parts of Scandinavia, including Jutland, whence comes the following case which I quote for the purpose of comparison.

### A CASE OF A MARA IN JUTLAND

Some reapers in a field, near a village in Jutland, came one evening upon a naked woman lying under a hedge, apparently asleep. Much surprised, they regarded her closely, and at length coming to the conclusion that her sleep was not natural, they summoned a shepherd who was generally regarded as very intelligent. On seeing the woman the shepherd at once said, "She is not a real person, though she looks like one. She is a mara, and has stripped for the purpose of riding some one to-night." At this there was loud laughter, and the reapers said, "Tell us another, Eric. A mara indeed! If this isn't a woman, our mothers are not women, for she is just as much of flesh and blood as they are." "All right," the shepherd replied, "wait and see." And bending over her, he whispered something in her ear, whereupon a queer little animal about two inches long came out of the grass, and running up her body, disappeared in her mouth. Then Eric pushed her, and she rolled over three times, then sprang to her feet, and with a wild startled cry leaped a high bush and disappeared. Nor could they, when they ran to the other side of the bush, find any traces of her.

Another recorded case is the following:

Christine Jansen had two lovers—Nielsen and Osdeven. Nielsen, who was a very good-looking young man, began to suffer from nightmare. He had the most appalling dreams of being strangled and suffocated, and they at last grew so frightful, and proved such a strain on his nerves, that he was forced to consult a doctor. The doctor attributed the cause to indigestion, and prescribed a special diet for him. But it was all of no avail; the bad dreams still continued, and Nielsen's health became more and more impaired.

At length, when he was almost worn out, having spent the greater part of many nights reading instead of sleeping, in order to avoid the frightful visions, he happened to mention his insufferable condition to Osdeven. Far from ridiculing his rival, Osdeven, with great earnestness, encouraged him to relate everything that had happened to him in his sleep; and when Nielsen had done so, exclaimed, "I'll tell you what it is—these dreams you have are not ordinary nightmares; they are due to a mara—I know their type well."

"To a mara!" Nielsen cried; "how ridiculous! Why not say to a mise—or—grim? It would be equally sensible; they are all idle superstitions."

"So you say now," Osdeven rejoined, "but wait! When you get into bed to-night, lie on your back, and in your right hand hold a sharp knife on your breast, the point upwards. Remain in this attitude from between eleven o'clock till two, and see what happens."

Nielsen laughed, but all the same decided to do as Osdeven suggested. Night came, and, knife in hand, he lay in his bed.

Minutes passed, and nothing happening, he was beginning to

think what a fool he was for wasting his time thus, when suddenly he perceived bending over him the luminous figure of a beautiful nude woman, whom, to his utter astonishment, he identified as Christine Jansen—Christine Jansen in all but expression. The expression in the eyes he now looked into was not human—it was hellish. The figure got on the bed and was in the act of sitting astride him, when it came in contact with the knife. Then it uttered a frightful scream of baffled rage and pain, and vanished.

Nielsen, shaking with terror and dreading another visitation, struck a light. The point of his knife was dripping with blood.

An hour later, overcome with weariness, he fell asleep, and for the first time for weeks his slumber was sound and undisturbed. Awaking in the morning much refreshed, he would have attributed his experience to imagination or to a dream, had it not been for the spots of blood on the bedclothes and the stains on his knife, and this evidence, as to the reality of what had happened, was strengthened by his discovery of certain circumstances in connexion with Miss Jansen, towards whom his sentiments had now undergone a complete change.

Curious to learn if anything had befallen her, he made cautious inquiries, and was informed that owing to a sudden indisposition—the nature of which was carefully hidden from him—she had been ordered abroad, where, in all probability, she would remain indefinitely.

Nielsen now had no more nightmare, and he and Osdeven, becoming firm friends, agreed that the next time they fell in love they would take good care it was not with a mara.

Another method of getting rid of maras was to sprinkle the air with sand, at the same time uttering a brief incantation. For example, in a village on the borders of Schleswig-Holstein, a woman who suffered agonies from nightmare consulted a man locally reported to be well versed in occult matters.

"Make your mind easy," said this man, after she had described her dreams to him; "I will soon put an end to your disturbances. It is a mara that is tormenting you. Don't be frightened if she suddenly manifests herself when I sprinkle this sand, for there will be nothing very alarming in her appearance, and she won't be able to harm you." He then proceeded to scatter several handfuls about the room, repeating as he did so a brief incantation.

He was still occupied thus, when, without a moment's warning, the figure of a very tall, naked woman appeared crouching on the bed. With a yell of rage she leaped on to the floor, her eyes flashing, and her lips twitching convulsively; and raising her hands as if she would like to scratch the incantator's face to pieces, she rushed furiously at him.

Far from being intimidated, however, he quite coolly dashed a handful of sand in her eyes, whereupon she instantly disappeared. "Now," he said, turning to the lady, who was half dead with terror, "you won't have the nightmare again"—which prophecy proved to be correct.

These instances will, I think, suffice to show the similarity between werwolves and maras. Both anomalies are dependent on properties of an entirely baneful nature; and both properties are either hereditary, having been established in families through the intercourse of those families in ages past with the superphysical Powers inimical to man; or are capable of being acquired through the practice of Black Magic.

## CHAPTER XV

# Werwolves in Norway and Sweden

**AS IN DENMARK**, werwolves were once so numerous in Norway and Sweden, that these countries naturally came to be regarded as the true home of lycanthropy.

With the advent of the tourist, however, and the consequent springing up of fresh villages, together with the gradual increase of native population, Norway and Sweden have slowly undergone a metamorphosis, with the result that it is now only in the most remote districts, such as the northern portion of the Kiolen Mountains and the borders of Lapland, that werwolves are to be found.

Here, amid the primitive solitude of vast pine forests, flow lycanthropous rivers; here, too, grow lycanthropous shrubs and flowers.

Werwolfery in Norway and Sweden is not confined to one sex; it is common to both; and in these countries various forms of spells, both for invoking and expelling lycanthropous spirits, are current.

As far as I can gather, a Norwegian or Swedish peasant, when he wishes to become a werwolf, kneels by the side of a lycanthropous stream at midnight, having chosen a night when the moon is in the full, and incants some such words as these:—

"'Tis night! 'tis night! and the moon shines white
Over pine and snow-capped hill;
The shadows stray through burn and brae
And dance in the sparkling rill.

"'Tis night! 'tis night! and the devil's light
Casts glimmering beams around.
The maras dance, the nisses prance
On the flower-enamelled ground.

"'Tis night! 'tis night! and the werwolf's might
Makes man and nature shiver.
Yet its fierce grey head and stealthy tread
Are nought to thee, oh river!
River, river, river.

"Oh water strong, that swirls along,
I prithee a werwolf make me.
Of all things dear, my soul, I swear,
In death shall not forsake thee."

The supplicant then strikes the banks of the river three times with his forehead; then dips his head into the river thrice, at each dip gulping down a mouthful of the water. This concludes the ceremony—he has become a werwolf, and twenty-four hours later will undergo the first metamorphosis.

Lycanthropous water is said, by those who dwell near to it, to differ from other water in subtle details only—details that would, in all probability, escape the notice of all who were not connoisseurs of the superphysical. A strange, faint odour, comparable with nothing, distinguishes lycanthropous water; there is a lurid sparkle in it, strongly suggestive of some peculiar, individual life; the noise it makes, as it rushes along, so closely resembles the muttering and whispering of human voices as to be often mistaken for them; whilst at night it sometimes utters piercing screams, and howls, and groans, in such a manner as to terrify all who pass near it. Dogs and horses, in particular, are susceptible to its influence, and they exhibit the greatest signs of terror at the mere sound of it.

Another means of becoming a werwolf, resorted to by the Swedish and Norwegian peasant, consists in the plucking and wearing of a lycanthropous flower after sunset, and on a night when the moon is in the full. Lycanthropous flowers, no less than lycanthropous water, possess properties peculiar to themselves; properties which are, probably, only discernible to those who are well acquainted with them. Their scent is described as faint and subtly suggestive of death, whilst their sap is rather offensively white and sticky. In appearance they are much the same as other flowers, and are usually white and yellow.

Yet another method of acquiring the property of lycanthropy consists in making: first, a magic circle on the ground, at twelve o'clock, on a night when the moon is in the full (there is no strict rule as to the magnitude of the circle, though one of about seven feet in diameter would seem to be the size most commonly adopted); then, in the centre of the circle, a wood fire, heating thereon an iron vessel containing one pint of clear spring water, and any seven of the following ingredients: hemlock (1/2 ounce to 1 ounce), aloe (30 grains), opium (2 to 4-1/2 drachms), mandrake (1 ounce to 1-1/2 ounces), solanum (1/2 ounce), poppy seed (1/2 ounce to 1 ounce), asafœtida (3/4 ounce to 1 ounce), and parsley (2 to 3 ounces).

Whilst the mixture is heating, the experimenter prostrates himself in front of the fire and prays to the Great Spirit of the Unknown to confer on him the property of metamorphosing, nocturnally, into a werwolf. His prayers take no one particular form, but are quite extempore; though he usually adds to them some such recognised incantation as:—

> "Come, spirit so powerful! come, spirit so dread,
> From the home of the werwolf, the home of the dead.
> Come, give me thy blessing! come, lend me thine ear!
> Oh spirit of darkness! oh spirit so drear!
>
> "Come, mighty phantom! come, great Unknown!
> Come from thy dwelling so gloomy and lone.
> Come, I beseech thee; depart from thy lair,
> And body and soul shall be thine, I declare.
>
> "Haste, haste, haste, horrid spirit, haste!
> Speed, speed, speed, scaring spirit, speed!
> Fast, fast, fast, fateful spirit, fast!"

He then makes the following formal declaration:—

> "I (here insert name) offer to thee, Great Spirit of the Unknown, this night (here insert date), my body and soul, on condition that thou grantest me, from this night to the hour of my death, the power of metamorphosing, nocturnally, into a wolf. I beg, I pray, I implore thee—thee, unparalleled Phantom of Darkness, to make me a werwolf—a werwolf!"

—and striking the ground three times with his forehead, he gets up. As soon as the concoction in the vessel is boiling, he dips a cup into it, and sprinkles the contents on the ground, repeating the action until he has sprinkled the whole interior of the circle.

Then he kneels on the ground close to the fire, and in a loud voice cries out, "Come, oh come!" and, if he is fortunate, a phantom suddenly manifests itself over the fire. Sometimes the phantom is indefinite—a cylindrical, luminous, pillar-like thing, about seven feet in height, having no discernible features; sometimes it assumes a definite shape, and appears either as a monstrous hooded figure with a death's head, or as a sub-human, sub-animal type of Elemental.

Whatever form the Unknown adopts, it is invariably terrifying. It never speaks, but indicates its assent by stretching out an arm, or what serves as an arm, and then disappears. It never remains visible for more than half a minute. As soon as it vanishes the supplicant, who is always half mad with terror, springs from the ground and rushes home—or anywhere to get again within reach of human beings. By the morning, however, all his fears have departed; and at sunset he creeps off into the forest, or into some equally secluded spot, to experience, for the first time, the extraordinary sensations of metamorphosing into a wolf, or, perhaps, a semi-wolf, *i.e.*, a creature half man and half wolf; for the degree of metamorphosis varies according to locality. The hour of metamorphosis also varies according to locality—though it is at sunset that the change most usually takes place, the transmutation back to man generally occurring at dawn.

When a werwolf, in human shape at the time, is killed, he sometimes (not always) metamorphoses into a wolf, and if in wolf's form at the time he is killed he sometimes (not always) metamorphoses into a human being—here again the nature of the transmutation depending on locality.

In certain of the forests of Sweden dwell old women called Vargamors, who are closely allied to werwolves, and exercise complete control over all the wolves in the neighbourhood, keeping the latter well supplied in food. As an illustration of the Vargamor I have chosen the following story:—

# LISO OF SOROA

Liso was thoroughly spoilt. Every one had told her how beautiful she was from the day she had first learned to walk, and, consequently, it was only natural that when she grew up she cared for no one but herself, and for nothing so much as gazing at herself in the looking-glass and expatiating on the loveliness of her own reflection. As a girl at home she was allowed to do precisely what she liked—neither father nor mother, relatives (with one exception) nor friends ever thwarted her; and when she married it was the same: her husband bowed down to her, and was always ready to indulge her every wish and whim.

She had three children, two boys and a girl, whom she occasionally condescended to notice; but only when there was nothing else at hand to entertain her.

The one person of whom Liso stood in awe was her aunt, a rich old lady with distinct views of her own, and a vigorous method of expressing them. Now, one of the old lady's peculiar ideas—at least peculiar in Liso's estimation—was that woman was made to be man's helpmate, and that married women should think of their husbands first, their children next, and themselves last—an order of consideration which Liso thought was exactly the reverse of what it should be.

Had her aunt been poor, it is quite certain that Liso would have had nothing whatsoever to do with her. But circumstances alter cases. This aunt was rich, and, moreover, had no one more nearly related to her than Liso.

One day, in the depth of winter, Liso received a letter from her aunt containing a pressing invitation to start off at once on a visit to the latter at Skatea, a small town some twelve miles from Soroa. "Bring your children," so the letter ran, "I should so love to see them, and stay the night." Liso was greatly annoyed. She had just arranged a meeting with one of her numerous lovers, and this invitation upset everything. However, as it was of vital importance to her to keep in with her aunt, she at once decided to put off her previous engagement and take her children to see their rich old relative.

Hoping that her lover might perhaps join her on the road and thus convert a boring journey into a pleasant pastime, Liso, in spite of her husband's entreaties, refused to take a servant, and insisted upon driving herself. As she had anticipated, her lover met her on the outskirts of the town, but, to her chagrin, was unable to accompany her any part of the way to Skatea. He was most profuse in his apologies, adding, "I wish you weren't going; I hear the road you will be traversing is infested with bears and wolves."

"Thank you!" she exclaimed mockingly, "I am not afraid, if you are. I can quite understand now why you cannot come. Good-bye!" And with a haughty inclination of her head she drove off, without deigning to notice the young man's outstretched hand. Liso was now in a very bad temper; and, having no other means of venting it, savagely silenced the children whenever they attempted to speak.

The vehicle in which the party travelled was a light sledge, drawn by one horse only—a beast of matchless beauty and size, which, under ordinary circumstances, could cover twelve miles in an almost inconceivably short space of time. But now, owing to a heavy fall of snow, the track, though well beaten, was heavy, and the piled-up snow on each side so deep that to turn back, without the risk of sticking fast, was an impossibility.

The first half of the journey passed without accident, and they were skirting the borders of a pine forest when Liso suddenly became conscious of a suspicious noise behind her. Looking round, she saw, to her horror, a troop of gaunt grey wolves issue from the forest and commence running after the sledge. She instantly slashed the horse with her whip, and the next moment the chase began in grim earnest. But, gallop as fast as it would, the horse could not outpace the wolves, whom hunger had made fleet as the wind, and it was not many minutes before two of the biggest of them appeared on either side of the vehicle. Though their intention was, in all probability, only to attack the horse, yet the safety both of Liso and the children depended on the preservation of the animal.

It was indeed a beautiful creature, and the danger only enhanced its value; it seemed, in fact, almost entitled to claim for its preservation an extraordinary sacrifice. And Liso did not hesitate. It was one life against three—the world would excuse her, if God did not.

"You, Charles," she said hoarsely, "you are the eldest; it is your duty to go first"—and before Charles had time to realize what was happening, she had gripped him round the waist, and with strength generated by the crisis hurled him into the snow. She did not see where he fell—the sledge was moving far too fast for that; but she heard the sound of the concussion, and then frantic screaming, accompanied by howls of triumph and joyful yapping. There was a momentary lull—only momentary—and then the patting footsteps recommenced.

Nearer and nearer they came, until she could hear a deep and regular pant, pant, pant, drowned every now and then by prolonged howls and piercing, nerve-racking whines. Once again two murder-breathing forms are racing along at the side of the sledge, biting and snapping at the horse's legs with their gleaming, foam-flecked jaws.

"George," Liso shouted, "you must go now. You are a boy, and boys and men should always die to save their sisters." But George, though younger, was not so easy to dispose of as Charles. Charles had been taken unawares, but George guessed what was coming and was on his guard.

"No, no," he cried, clinging on to the sledge with both his chubby hands. "The wolves will eat me! Take sissy."

"Wretch!" shrieked Liso, boxing his ears furiously. "Selfish little wretch! So this is the result of all the kindness I have lavished on you. Let go at once"—and tearing at his baby wrists with all her might, she succeeded in loosening them, and the next instant he was in the road.

Then there was a repetition of what had happened before—a few wild screeches, savage howls of triumph, and snarls and grunts that suggested much. Then—comparative quiet, and then—patterings. Mad with fear, Liso stood up and lashed the horse. God of mercy! there was now only one more life between hers and the fate that, of all fates in the world, seemed to her just then to be the most dreadful. With the thick and gloomy forest before and behind her, and the nearer and nearer trampling of her ravenous pursuers, she almost collapsed from sheer anguish; but the thought of all her beauty perishing in such an ignominious and painful fashion braced her up. Perhaps, too—at least, let us hope so—underlying it all, though so much in the background, there was a genuine longing to save the little mite—her exact counterpart, so people said—that nestled its sunny head in the folds of her soft and costly sealskin coat.

She did not venture to look behind her, only in front—at the seemingly never-ending white track; at the dense mass of trees—trees that shook their heads mockingly at her as the wind rustled through them; at the great splash of red right across the sky, so horribly remindful of blood that she shuddered. Night birds hoot; wild cats glare down at her; and shadows of every kind glide noiselessly out from behind the great trunks, and await her approach with inexplicable flickerings and flutterings.

All at once two rough paws are laid on her shoulders, and the wide-open, bloody jaws of an enormous wolf hang over her head. It is the most ferocious beast of the troop, which, having partly missed its leap at the sledge, is dragged along with it, in vain seeking with its hinder legs for a resting-place to enable it to get wholly on to the frail vehicle. Liso looks down at the little girl beside her and their eyes meet.

"Not me! not me!" the tiny one cried, clutching hold of her wrist in its anxiety. "I have been good, have I not? You will not throw me into the snow like the others?" Liso's lips tightened. The weight of the body of the wolf drew her gradually backwards—another minute and she would be out of the sledge. Her life was of assuredly more value than that of the child. Besides, one so young would not feel the horrors of death so acutely as she would, who was grown up. Anything rather than such a devilish ending. Providence willed it—Providence must bear the responsibility. And, steeling her soul to pity, she snatches up her daughter and throws her into the gleaming jaws of the wolf, which, springing off the sledge, hastily departs with its prey into the forest, where it is followed by hosts of other wolves. Exhausted, stunned, senseless—for her escape has been extremely narrow—Liso drops the reins, and, sinking back into the luxurious cushions of the vehicle, gives a great sigh of relief and shuts her eyes.

Meantime the trees grow thinner, and an isolated house, to which a side-road leads, appears at no great distance off. The horse, left to itself, follows this new path; it enters through an open gate, and, panting and foaming, comes to a dead halt before a ponderous oak door studded with huge iron nails. Presently Liso recovers. She finds herself seated before a roaring fire; and a woman with a white face, dark, piercing eyes, and a beak-like nose, is bending over her. The woman presents such an extraordinary spectacle that Liso is oblivious of everything else, and gazes at her with a cold sensation of fear creeping down her spine.

"You've had a narrow escape," the woman presently exclaims in peculiarly hoarse tones. "And the danger is not over yet! Listen!" To Liso's terror an inferno of howls and whines sounds from the yard outside, and she sees, gleaming in at her through the window-panes, scores of wild, hairy faces with pale, lurid eyes. "They are there!" the woman remarks, a saturnine smile in her eyes and playing round her lips. "There—all ready to rend and tear you to pieces as they did your children—your three pretty, loving children. I've only to open the door, and in they will rush!"

"But you won't," Liso gasped feebly. "You won't be so cruel. Besides, they could eat you, too."

"Oh no, they couldn't," the woman laughed. "I'm a Vargamor. Every one of these wolves knows me and loves me as a mother. With you it is very different. Shall I——?"

"Oh no! for pity's sake spare me!" Liso cried, throwing herself at the woman's feet and catching hold of her hands. "Spare me, and I will do anything you want."

"Well," said the woman, after some consideration, "I will spare you on one condition, namely, that you live with me and do the housework; I'm getting too old for it."

"I suppose I may see my family occasionally?" Liso said.

"No!" the old woman snapped, "you may not. You must never go out of sight of this house. Now, what do you say? Recollect, it is either that or the wolves! Quick," and she hobbled to the door as she spoke.

"I've chosen!" Liso shrieked. "I'll stay with you. Anything rather than such an awful death. Tell me what I have to do and I'll begin at once."

The old woman took her at her word. She speedily set Liso a task, and from that time onward, kept her so continuously employed, not allowing her a moment to herself, that her life soon became unbearable. She tried to escape, but each time she left the house the fierce howling of the wolves sent her back to it in terror, and she discovered that, night and day, certain of the beasts were supervising her movements. After she had been there a week the old woman said to her, "I fear it is useless to think of keeping you any longer! Times are bad—food is scarce. The wolves are hungry—I must give you to them."

But Liso fell on her knees and pleaded so hard that the Vargamor relented, "Well, well!" she said, "I will spare you, provided you can procure me a substitute. If you like to sit down and write to some one I will see that the note is delivered."

Then Liso, almost beside herself at the thought of the hungry wolves, sat down and wrote a letter to her husband, telling him she had met with an accident, and desiring him to come to her at once. She dared not give him the slightest hint as to what had actually befallen her, as she knew the old woman would read the letter.

When she had finished her note, the Vargamor took it, and for the next twelve hours Liso had a very anxious time.

"If he doesn't come soon," the old woman at length said to her, with an evil chuckle, "I shall have to let the wolves in. They are famishing; and I, too, want something tastier than rabbits and squirrels."

The minutes passed, and Liso was nearly fainting with suspense, when there suddenly broke on her ears the distant tramp of horses' feet; and in a very few moments a droshky dashed up to the door.

"Call him in here," the Vargamor said, "and run up and hide in your bedroom. My pets and I will enjoy him all the better by the fire, and there won't be so much risk of them being hurt."

Liso, afraid to do otherwise, ran up the rickety ladder leading to her room, shouting as she did so, "Oscar! Oscar! come in, come in."

The joyful note in her husband's voice as he replied to her

invitation struck a new chord in Liso's nature—a chord which had been there all the time, but had got choked and clogged through over-indulgence. Full of a courage that dared anything in its determination to save him, she crept cautiously down the stairs, and just as he crossed the threshold, and the Vargamor was about to summon the wolves, she dashed up to the old woman and struck her with all her might. Then, seizing her husband, she dragged him out of the house, and, hustling him into the carriage, jumped in by his side and told the coachman to drive home with the utmost speed.

All this was done in less time than it takes to tell, and once again the familiar sounds of pattering—patterings on the snow in the wake of the carriage—fell on Liso's ears, and all the old horrors of the preceding journey came back to her with full force.

Slowly, despite the fact that there were two horses now, the wolves gained on them, and once again the same harrowing question arose in Liso's mind. Some one must be sacrificed. Which should it be? The coachman! without doubt the coachman. He was only a poor, uneducated man, a hireling, and his life was as nothing compared either with that of her husband or her own.

But she now remembered that Oscar, though usually a mere straw in her hands, and ready to do anything she asked him, had one or two peculiarities—fondness for children and animals, and a great respect for life—life in every grade. Would he consent to sacrifice the coachman? And as she glanced at him, a feeling of awe came over her. What a big, strong man this husband of hers was, and what strength he had—strength of all kinds, physical as well as mental—if he cared to exert it. But then he loved, worshipped, and adored her;

he would never treat her with anything but the utmost deference and kindness, no matter what she said or did. Still, when she got ready to whisper the fatal suggestion in his ear, her heart failed her. And then the new something within her—that something that had already spoken and seemed inclined to be painfully officious—once more asserted itself. The coachman was married, he had children—four people dependent on him, four hearts that loved him! With her it was different: no one was actually dependent on her—there were no children now! Nothing but the memory of them! Memory—what a hateful thing it was! She had forced them to give her their lives; would it not be some atonement for her act if she were now to offer hers? She made the offer—breathed it with a shuddering soul into her husband's ears—and with a great round oath he rejected it.

"What! You! Let you be thrown to the wolves?" he roared. "No—sooner than that, ten thousand times sooner, I will jump out! But I don't think there is any need. Knowing there were wolves about, I brought arms. If occasion arises we can easily account for half of them. But we shall outdistance them yet."

He spoke the truth. Bit by bit the powerful horses drew away from the pack, and ere the last trees of the forest were passed, the howlings were no longer heard and all danger was at an end.

Then, and not till then, did Oscar learn what had become of the children.

He listened to Liso's explanation in silence, and it was not until she had finished that the surprise came. She was anticipating commiseration—commiseration for the awful hell she had undergone. She little guessed the struggle that was taking place beneath her husband's seemingly calm exterior. The revelation came with an abruptness that staggered her. "Woman!" he cried, "you are a murderess. Sooner than have sacrificed your children you should have suffered three deaths yourself—that is the elementary instinct of all mothers, human and otherwise. You are below the standard of a beast—of the Vargamor you slew. Go! go back to those parents who bore you, and tell them I'll have nought to do with you—that I want a woman for my wife, not a monstrosity."

He bade the coachman pull up, and, alighting, told the man to drive Liso to the home of her parents.

But Liso did not hear him—she sat huddled up on the seat with her eyes staring blankly before her. For the first time in her life she was conscious that she loved!

CHAPTER XVI

# Werwolves in Iceland, Lapland, and Finland

THE BERSEKIR OF Iceland are credited with the rare property of dual metamorphosis—that is to say, they are credited with the power of being able to adopt the individual forms of two animals—the bear and the wolf.

For substantiation as to the *bona-fide* existence of this rare property of dual metamorphosis one has only to refer to the historical literature of the country (the authenticity of which is beyond dispute), wherein many cases of it are recorded.

The following story, illustrative of dual metamorphosis, was told to me on fairly good authority.

A very unprepossessing Bersekir, named Rerir, falling in love with Signi, the beautiful daughter of a neighbouring Bersekir, proposed to her and was scornfully rejected. Smarting under the many insults that had been heaped on him—for Signi had a most cutting tongue—Rerir, who, like most of the Bersekir, was both a werwolf and a wer-bear, resolved to be revenged. Assuming the shape of a bear—the animal he deemed the more formidable—Rerir stole to the house where Signi and her parents lived, and climbing on the roof, tore away at it with his claws till he had made a hole big enough to admit him. Dropping through the aperture he had thus effected, he alighted on the top of some one in bed—one of the servants of the house—whom he hugged to death before she had time to utter a cry. He then stole out into the passage and made his way, cautiously and noiselessly, to the room in which he imagined Signi slept. Here, however, instead of finding the object of his passions, he came upon her parents, one of whom—the mother—was awake; and aiming a blow at the latter's head, he crushed in her skull with one stroke of his powerful paw. The noise awoke Signi's father, who, taking in the situation at a glance, also metamorphosed into a bear and straightway closed with his assailant. A desperate encounter between the two wer-animals now commenced, and the whole household, aroused from their slumber, came trooping in. For some time the issue of the combat was dubious, both adversaries being fairly well matched. But at length Rerir began to prevail, and Signi's father cried out for some one to help him. Then Signi, anxious to save her parent's life, seized a knife, and, aiming a frantic blow, inadvertently struck her father, who instantly sank on the ground, leaving her at the mercy of his furious opponent.

With a loud snarl of triumph, Rerir rushed at the girl, and was bearing her triumphantly away, when the cook—an old woman who had followed the fortunes of the Bersekir all her life—had a sudden inspiration. Standing on a shelf in the corner of the room was a jar containing a preparation of sulphur, asafœtida, and castoreum, which her mistress had always given her to understand was a preventive against evil spirits. Snatching it up, she darted after the wer-bear and flung the contents of it in its face, just as it was about to descend the stairs with Signi. In a moment there was a sudden and startling metamorphosis, and in the place of the bear stood the ugly, misshapen man, Rerir.

The hunchback now would gladly have departed without attempting further mischief; for although the household boasted no man apart from its incapacitated master, there were still three formidable women and some big dogs to be faced.

But to let him escape, after the irreparable harm he had done, was the very last thing Signi would permit; and with an air of stern authority she commanded the servants to fall on him with any weapons they could find, whilst she would summon the hounds.

Now, indeed, the tables were completely turned. Rerir was easily overpowered and bound securely hand and foot by Signi and her servants, and after undergoing a brief trial the following morning he was summarily executed.

Those Icelanders who possessed the property of metamorphosis into wolves and bears (they were always of the male sex), more often than not used it for the purpose of either wreaking vengeance or of executing justice. The terrible temper—for the rage of the Bersekir has been a byword for centuries—commonly attributed to Icelanders and Scandinavians in general, is undoubtedly traceable to the werwolves and wer-bears into which the Bersekirs metamorphosed.

It is said that in Iceland there are both lycanthropous streams and flowers, and that they differ little if at all from those to be met with in other countries.

## THE WERWOLVES OF LAPLAND

In Lapland werwolves are still much to the fore. In many families the property is hereditary, whilst it is not infrequently sought and acquired through the practice of Black Magic. Though, perhaps, more common among males, there are, nevertheless, many instances of it among females.

The following case comes from the country bordering on Lake Enara.

The child of a peasant woman named Martha, just able to trot alone, and consequently left to wander just where it pleased, came home one morning with its forehead apparently licked raw, all its fingers more or less injured, and two of them seemingly sucked and mumbled to a mere pulp.

On being interrogated as to what had happened, it told a most astounding tale: A very beautiful lady had picked it up and carried it away to her house, where she had put it in a room with her three children, who were all very pretty and daintily dressed. At sunset, however, both the lady and her children metamorphosed into wolves, and would undoubtedly have eaten it, had they not satiated their appetites on a portion of a girl which had been kept over from the preceding day. The newcomer was intended for their meal on the morrow, and obeying the injunctions of their mother, the young werwolves had forborne to devour the child, though they had all tasted it.

The child's parents were simply dumbfounded—they could scarcely credit their senses—and made their offspring repeat its narrative over and over again. And as it stuck to what it had said, they ultimately concluded that it was true, and that the lady described could be none other than Madame Tonno, the wife of their landlord and patron—a person of immense importance in the neighbourhood.

But what could they do? How could they protect their children from another raid?

To accuse the lady, who was rich and influential, of being a werwolf would be useless. No one would believe them—no one dare believe them—and they would be severely punished for their indiscretion. Being poor, they were entirely at her mercy, and if she chose to eat their children, they could not prevent her, unless they could catch her in the act.

One evening the mother was washing clothes before the door of her house, with her second child, a little girl of four years of age, playing about close by. The cottage stood in a lonely part of the estate, forming almost an island in the midst of low boggy ground; and there was no house nearer than that of M. Tonno. Martha, bending over her wash-tub, was making every effort to complete her task, when a fearful cry made her look up, and there was the child, gripped by one shoulder, in the jaws of a great she-wolf, the arm that was free extended towards her. Martha was so close that she managed to clutch a bit of the child's clothing in one hand, whilst with the other she beat the brute with all her might to make it let go its hold. But all in vain: the relentless jaws did not show the slightest sign of relaxing, and with a saturnine glitter in its deep-set eyes it emitted a hoarse burr-burr, and set off at full speed towards the forest, dragging the mother, who was still clinging to the garment of her child, with it.

But they did not long continue thus. The wolf turned into some low-lying uneven track, and Martha, falling over the jagged trunk of a tree, found herself lying on the ground with only a little piece of torn clothing tightly clasped in her hand. Hitherto, comforted by Martha's presence, the little one had not uttered a sound; but now, feeling itself deserted, it gave vent to the most heartrending screams—screams that abruptly disturbed the silence of that lonely spot and pierced to the depths of Martha's soul. In an instant she rose, and, dashing on, bounded over stock and stone, tearing herself pitiably, but heeding it not in her intense anxiety to save her child. But the wolf had now increased its speed; the undergrowth was thick, the ground heavier, and soon screams became her only guide. Still on and on she dashed, now snatching up a little shoe which was clinging to the bushes, now shrieking with agony as she saw fragments of the child's hair and clothes on the low jagged boughs obstructing her path. On, on, on, until the screams grew fainter, then louder, and then ceased altogether.

Late that night the husband, Max, found his wife lying dead, just outside the grounds of his patron's château. Guessing what had happened, and having but one thought in his mind—namely, revenge—Max, arming himself with the branch of a tree, marched boldly up to the house, and rapped loudly at the door.

M. Tonno answered this peremptory summons himself, and demanded in an angry voice what Max meant by daring to announce himself thus.

Max pointed in the direction of the corpse. "That!" he shrieked; "that is the reason of my visit. Madame Tonno is a werwolf—she has murdered both my wife and child, and I am here to demand justice."

"Come inside," M. Tonno said, the tone of his voice suddenly changing. "We can discuss the matter indoors in the privacy of my study." And he conducted Max to a room in the rear of the house.

But no sooner had Max crossed the threshold than the door was slammed on him, and he found himself a prisoner. He turned to the window, but there was no hope there—it was heavily barred. But although a peasant—and a fool, so he told himself, to have thus deliberately walked into a trap—Max was not altogether without wits, and he searched the room thoroughly, eventually discovering a loose board. Tearing it up, he saw that the space under the floor—that is to say, between the floor and the foundation of the house—was just deep enough for him to lie there at full length. Here, then, was a possible avenue of escape. Setting to work, he succeeded, after much effort, in wrenching up another board, and then another, and getting into the excavation thus made, he worked his way along on his stomach, until he came to a grating, which, to his utmost joy, proved to be loose. It was but the work of a few minutes to force it out and to dislodge a few bricks, and Max was once again free. His one idea now was to tell his tale to his brother peasants and rouse them to immediate action, and with this end in view he set off running at full speed to the nearest settlement.

The peasants of Lapland are slow and stolid and take a lot of rousing, but when once they are roused, few people are so terrible.

Fortunately for Max, he was not the only sufferer; several other people in the neighbourhood had lately lost their children, and the story he told found ready credence. In less than an hour a large body of men and women, armed with every variety of weapon, from a sword to a pitchfork, had gathered together, and setting off direct to the château, they surrounded it on all sides, and forcing an entrance, seized M. Tonno and his werwolf wife and werwolf children, and binding them hand and foot, led them to the shores of Lake Enara and drowned them. They then went back to the house and, setting fire to it, burned it to the ground, thus making certain of destroying any werwolf influence it might still contain.

With this wholesale extermination a case that may be taken as a characteristic type of Lapland lycanthropy in all its grim and sordid details concludes.

## FINLAND WERWOLVES

Finland teems with stories of werwolves—stories ancient and modern, for the werwolf is said to still flourish in various parts of the country.

The property is not restricted to one sex; it is equally common to both. Spells and various forms of exorcism are used, and certain streams are held to be lycanthropous.

However, in Finland as in Scandinavia, it is very difficult to procure information as to werwolves. The common peasant, who alone knows anything about the anomaly, is withheld by superstition from even mentioning its name; and if he mentions a werwolf at all, designates him only as the "old one," or the "grey one," or the "great dog," feeling that to call this terror by its true name is a sure way to exasperate it. It is only by strategy one learns from a peasant that when a fine young ox is found in the morning breathing hard, his hide bathed in foam, and with every sign of fright and exhaustion, while, perhaps, only one trifling wound is discovered on the whole body, which swells and inflames as if poison had been infused, the animal generally dying before night; and that when, on examination of the corpse, the intestines are found to be torn as with the claws of a wolf, and the whole body is in a state of inflammation, it is accounted certain that the mischief has been caused by a werwolf.

It is thus a werwolf serves his quarry when he kills for the mere love of killing, and not for food.

In Finland, perhaps more than in other countries, werwolves are credited with demoniacal power, and old women who possess the property of metamorphosing into wolves are said to be able to paralyse cattle and children with their eyes, and to have poison in their nails, one wound from which causes certain death.

To illustrate the foregoing I have selected an incident which happened near Diolen, a village on the eastern shore of the Gulf of Finland, at the distance of about a hundred wersts from the ancient city of Mawa. Here vegetation is of a more varied and luxuriant kind than is usually found in the Northern latitude; the oak and the bela, intermingled with rich plots of grass, grow at the very edge of the sea—a phenomenon accountable for by the fact that the Baltic is tideless.

For about half a werst in breadth, the shore continues a level, luxuriant stretch, when it suddenly rises in three successive cliffs, each about a hundred feet in height, and placed about the same space of half a werst, one behind the other, like huge steps leading to the table-land above. In some places the rocks are completely hidden from the view by a thick fence of trees, which take root at their base, while each level is covered by a minute forest of firs, in which grow a variety of herbs and shrubs, including the English whitethorn, and wild strawberries.

It was to gather the latter that Savanich and his seven-year-old son, Peter, came one afternoon early in summer. They had filled two baskets and were contemplating returning home with their spoil, when Caspan, the big sheepdog, uttered a low growl.

"Hey, Caspan, what is it?" Peter cried. "Footsteps! And such curious ones!"

"They are curious," Savanich said, bending down to examine them. "They are larger and coarser than those of Caspan, longer in shape, and with a deep indentation of the ball of the foot. They are those of a wolf—an old one, because of the deepness of the tracks. Old wolves walk heavy. And here's a wound the brute has got in its paw. See! there is a slight irregularity on the print of the hind feet, as if from a dislocated claw. We must be on our guard. Wolves are hungry now: the waters have driven them up together, and the cattle are not let out yet. The beast is not far off, either. An old wolf like this will prowl about for days together, round the same place, till he picks up something."

"I hope it won't attack us, father," Peter said, catching hold of Savanich by the hand. "What should you do if it did?"

But before Savanich could reply, Caspan gave a loud bark and dashed into the thicket, and the next moment a terrible pandemonium of yells, and snorts, and sharp howls filled the air. Drawing his knife from its sheath, and telling Peter to keep close at his heels, Savanich followed Caspan and speedily came upon the scene of the encounter. Caspan had hold of a huge grey wolf by the neck, and was hanging on to it like grim death, in spite of the brute's frantic efforts to free itself.

There was but little doubt that the brave dog would have, eventually, paid the penalty for its rashness—for the wolf had mauled it badly, and it was beginning to show signs of exhaustion through loss of blood—had not Savanich arrived in the nick of time. A couple of thrusts from his knife stretched the wolf on the ground, when, to his utmost horror, it suddenly metamorphosed into a hideous old hag.

"A werwolf!" Savanich gasped, crossing himself. "Get out of her way, Peter, quick!"

But it was too late. Thrusting out a skinny hand, the hag scratched Peter on the ankle with the long curved, poisonous nail of her forefinger. Then, with an evil smile on her lips, she turned over on her back, and expired. And before Peter could be got home he, too, was dead.

## CHAPTER XVII
## The Werwolf in Russia and Siberia

THE IDEAL HOME of all things weird and uncanny—is cold, grey, gaunt, and giant Russia. Nowhere is the werwolf so much in evidence to-day as in the land of the Czar, where all the primitive conditions favourable to such anomalies, still exist, and where they have undergone but little change in the last ten thousand years.

A thinly-populated country—vast stretches of wild uncultivated land, full of dense forests, rich in trees most favourable to Elementals, and watered by deep, silent tarns, and stealthily moving streams,—its very atmosphere is impregnated with lycanthropy.

At the base of giant firs and poplars, or poking out their heads impudently, from amidst brambles and ferns, are werwolf flowers—flowers with all the characteristics of those found in Hungary and the Balkan Peninsula, but of a greater variety. There are, for example, in addition to the white, yellow, and red species, those of a bluish-white hue, that emit a glow at night like the phosphorescent glow emanating from decaying animal and vegetable matter; and those of a brilliant orange, covered with black, protruding spots, suggestive of some particularly offensive disease, that show a marked preference for damp places, and are specially to be met with growing in the slime and mud at the edge of a pool, or in the soft, rotten mould of morasses.

Werwolves haunt the plains, too—the great barren, undulating deserts that roll up to the foot of the Urals, Caucasus, Altai, Yablonoi, and Stanovoi Mountains—and the Tundras along the shores of the Arctic Ocean—dreary swamps in summer and ice-covered wastes in winter. Here, at night, they wander over the rough, stony, arid ground, picking their way surreptitiously through the scant vegetation, and avoiding all frequented localities; pausing, every now and then, to slake their thirst in deep sunk wells, or to listen for the sounds of quarry. Hazel hen, swans, duck, geese, squirrels, hares, elk, reindeer, roes, fallowdeer, and wild sheep, all are food to the werwolf, though nothing is so heartily appreciated by it as fat tender children or young and plump women.

In its nocturnal ramblings the werwolf often encounters enemies—bears, wolves, and panthers—with which it struggles for dominion—dominion of forest, plain and mountain; and when the combat ends to its disadvantage, its metamorphosed corpse is at once devoured by its conqueror.

Of all parts of Russia, the werwolf loves best the Caucasus and Ural Mountains. They are to Russia what the Harz Mountains were to Germany, centuries ago—the head-quarters of all manner of psychic phenomena, the happy hunting ground of phantom and fairy; and over them still lingers, almost, if not quite, as forcibly as ever, the glamour and mystery inseparable from the superphysical.

Times without number have the great black beetling crags of

these mountains been scaled by the furry, sinewy feet of werwolves; times without number have the shadows of these anomalies fallen on the moon-kissed, snowy peaks, towering high into the sky, or mingled with the rank and dewy herbage in the pine-clad valleys, and narrow abysmal gorges deep down below.

It was here, in these lone Russian mountains, so legend relates, that Peter and Paul turned an impious wife and husband, who refused them shelter, into wolves: but Peter and Paul, apparently, had not the monopoly of this power; for it was here, too, in a Ural village, that the Devil is alleged to have metamorphosed half a dozen men into wolves for not paying him sufficient homage.

There is no restriction as to the sex of werwolves in Russia and Siberia—male and female werwolves are about equal in number, though perhaps there is a slight preponderance in favour of the female. Vargamors are to be encountered in almost all the less frequented woody regions, but more especially in those in the immediate vicinity of the Urals and Caucasus.

Though many of the werwolves inherit the property, many, too, have acquired it through direct intercourse with the superphysical; and the invocation of spirits, whether performed individually or collectively, is far from uncommon.

Black Magic is said to be practised in the Urals, Caucasus, Yerkhoiansk, and Stanovoi Mountains; in the Tundras, the Plains of East Russia, the Timan Range, the Kola Peninsula, and various parts of Siberia.

I am told that the usual initiating ceremony consists of drawing a circle, from seven to nine feet in radius, in the centre of which circle a wood fire is kindled—the wood selected being black poplar, pine or larch, never ash. A fumigation in an iron vessel, heated over the fire, is then made out of a mixture of any four or five of the following substances: Hemlock (2 to 3 ounces), henbane (1 ounce to 1-1/2 ounces), saffron (3 ounces), poppy seed (any amount), aloe (3 drachms), opium (1/4 ounce), asafœtida (2 ounces), solanum (2 to 3 drachms), parsley (any amount).

As soon as the vessel is placed over the fire so that it can heat, the person who would invoke the spirit that can bestow upon him the property of metamorphosing into a wolf kneels within the circle, and prays a preliminary impromptu prayer. He then resorts to an incantation, which runs, so I have been told, as follows:—

"Hail, hail, hail, great wolf spirit, hail!
A boon I ask thee, mighty shade.
Within this circle I have made,
Make me a werwolf strong and bold,
The terror alike of young and old.
Grant me a figure tall and spare;
The speed of the elk, the claws of the bear;
The poison of snakes, the wit of the fox;
The stealth of the wolf, the strength of the ox;
The jaws of the tiger, the teeth of the shark;
The eyes of a cat that sees in the dark.
Make me climb like a monkey, scent like a dog,
Swim like a fish, and eat like a hog.
Haste, haste, haste, lonely spirit, haste!
Here, wan and drear, magic spell making,
Findest thou me—shaking, quaking.
Softly fan me as I lie,
And thy mystic touch apply—
Touch apply, and I swear that when I die,
When I die, I will serve thee evermore,
Evermore, in grey wolf land, cold and raw."

The incantation concluded, the supplicant then kisses the ground three times, and advancing to the fire, takes off the iron vessel, and whirling it smoking round his head, cries out:—

> "Make me a werwolf! make me a man-eater!
> Make me a werwolf! make me a woman-eater!
> Make me a werwolf! make me a child-eater!
> I pine for blood! human blood!
> Give it me! give it me to-night!
> Great Wolf Spirit! give it me, and
> Heart, body, and soul, I am yours."

The trees then begin to rustle, and the wind to moan, and out of the sudden darkness that envelops everything glows the tall, cylindrical, pillar-like phantom of the Unknown, seven or eight feet in height. It sometimes develops further, and assumes the form of a tall, thin monstrosity, half human and half animal, grey and nude, with very long legs and arms, and the feet and claws of a wolf. Its head is shaped like that of a wolf, but surrounded with the hair of a woman, that falls about its bare shoulders in yellow ringlets. It has wolf's ears and a wolf's mouth. Its aquiline nose and pale eyes are fashioned like those of a human being, but animated with an expression too diabolically malignant to proceed from anything but the superphysical.

It seldom if ever speaks, but either utters some extraordinary noise—a prolonged howl that seems to proceed from the bowels of the earth, a piercing, harrowing whine, or a low laugh full of hellish glee, any of which sounds may be taken to express its assent to the favour asked.

It only remains visible for a minute at the most, and then disappears with startling abruptness. The supplicant is now a werwolf. He undergoes his first metamorphosis into wolf form the following evening at sunset, reassuming his human shape at dawn; and so on, day after day, till his death, when he may once more metamorphose either from man form to wolf form, or vice versa, his corpse retaining whichever form has been assumed at the moment of death. However, with regard to this final metamorphosis there is no consistency: it may or may not take place. In the practice of exorcism, for the purpose of eradicating the evil property of werwolfery, all manner of methods are employed. Sometimes the werwolf is soundly whipped with ash twigs, and saturated with a potion such as I described in a previous chapter; sometimes he is made to lie or sit over, or lie or stand close beside, a vessel containing a fumigation mixture composed of sulphur, asafœtida, and castoreum, or hypericum and vinegar; or sometimes, again, he is well whipped and rubbed all over with the juice of the mistletoe berry. Occasionally a priest is summoned, and then a formal ceremony takes place.

An altar is erected. On it are placed lighted candles, a Bible, a crucifix. The werwolf, in wolf form, bound hand and foot, is then placed on the ground at the foot of the altar, and fumigated with incense and sprinkled with holy water. The sign of the cross is made on his forehead, chest, back, and on the palms of his hands. Various prayers are read, and the affair concludes when the priest in a loud voice adjures the evil influence to depart, in the name of God the Father, the Son, the Holy Ghost, and the Virgin Mary.

I have never, however, heard of any well-authenticated case testifying to the efficacy of this or of any other mode of exorcism. As far as I know, once a werwolf always a werwolf is an inviolable rule.

Apparently women are more desirous of becoming werwolves than men, more women than men having acquired the property of werwolfery through their own act. In the case of women candidates for this evil property, the inspiring motive is almost always one of revenge, sometimes on a faithless lover, but more often on another woman; and when once women metamorphose thus, their craving for human flesh is simply insatiable—in fact, they are far more cruel and daring, and much more to be dreaded, than male werwolves. The following story seems to bear out the truth of this assertion:—

## THE CASE OF IVAN OF SHIGANSKA

Shiganska was—for it no longer exists, having been obliterated about fifty years ago by a blizzard—a small village on the left bank of the Petchora, about a hundred miles from its mouth.

Owing chiefly to the character of the adjacent country, Shiganska was wanting in every beauty and variety that charms the eye. It was situated on a stretch of flat land between two mountain ranges, *i.e.*, the Ural on one side and the Taman on the other, and surrounded by a wood so thick that it was with the greatest difficulty anyone could force a way into it, supposing they had been sufficiently fortunate to escape sticking fast in the morasses of soft, rotten mould, that lie hidden in the least suspicious looking places, on its borders. Here were to be found lycanthropous blue and white flowers, which those desirous of becoming werwolves sought from far and wide, some even coming from Siberia, and some from away down South as far as Astrakan. And the woods abounded not only in werwolves, but in all sorts of supernatural horrors—phantoms of the dead, *i.e.* (of murderers and suicides) Vice Elementals and Vagrarians, vampires and ghouls; no region in Russia boasted so many, and for this reason it was scrupulously avoided by all sensible people after sunset.

Ivan, like most of the male inhabitants of Shiganska, lived by the chase: the black fox, the sable, the fox with the dark-coloured throat, the red fox, white fox, squirrel, ermine, and black bear alike fell victims to his gun; whilst in the Petchora, when the weather permitted it, he caught, besides many other kinds of fish, a goodly proportion of salmon, nelma (a kind of salmon trout), bleak, sturgeon, sterlet, tochü, muksun, omul, and *Salmo Lavaretus*.

It was a good living, that of the chase, albeit fraught with grave dangers; and Ivan, thanks to his exceptional powers with the rod as well as the rifle, was on the high road to prosperity.

He lived with his mother and two sisters in a pretty house about a kös from Shiganska, and facing it was a level stretch of reed-grass terminating in the hemlock-covered banks of the Petchora. A few trees, chiefly birch and larch, dotted about the reed-grass afforded a delightful shade from the fierce heat of the short summer sun; and birds of all sorts, whose singing was a source of the keenest delight to Ivan and his sisters, made their homes in them.

Unlike any other hunter in Shiganska, Ivan was fond of poetry and music; moreover, he had a dreamy disposition, and when his day's work was done he was content—nay, more than content—to watch the changing colours in the sky, or see in the glowing embers of the charcoal fire strange scenes and wildly familiar faces.

One morning, in the month of April, Ivan set off to the woods, gun in hand, accompanied by his old and faithful dog, Dolk, in search of big game. He paused every now and then to look at the ice on the summits of the distant mountains. The sunlight falling on it imparted to it many different hues, and made it sparkle like flaming jewels. He stopped repeatedly to listen to the croaking of the raven, the cawing of the crows, and the piping of the bullfinches—sounds of which he was never weary, and never tired of trying to interpret.

On this occasion, as usual, it was not until long after noon that he began seriously to think of looking for his quarry, and it was not until he had searched for some time that he at length came upon the tracks of a wild reindeer. Loosing Dolk, and tightening the buckles of his snow-shoes, he set to work to stalk the animal, and eventually sighted it browsing on a clump of reed-grass that grew on the bank of a mountain stream. The chase now began in earnest. It was a beautiful animal, and Ivan strained every effort to get within shooting range by leaping from rock to rock, and springing over stream after stream. In this manner he had progressed for more than a kös, when blood from the feet of the reindeer began to be visible on the fresh frozen snow; from its faltering pace the poor creature was evidently tired out, and Dolk was drawing closer and closer to it. In these circumstances Ivan was counting on the likelihood of his soon being near enough to fire, when suddenly the joyful barking of the dog changed to a prodigious howl of agony. With redoubled speed Ivan pushed ahead, and, presently, at a distance of about two gunshots, he saw two small black objects lying on the snow covered with blood.

They were the remains of Dolk, who, having come up with the reindeer and driven it into a small brook, was keeping it there until Ivan arrived, when a hungry wolf had leaped down the side of a rock and, seizing him in his powerful jaws, had bitten him in half. The wolf had evidently intended to eat Dolk, but, catching sight of Ivan, had made off.

Ivan was inconsolable. Dolk had hunted with him as a puppy of six months old, and for eight years the dog had never let him know a hungry day. Ivan had been offered ten reindeer for him, but he would not have parted with him for any number, and without Dolk he knew not how to show himself at home, for both his mother and sisters were devoted to the faithful animal.

Determined on vengeance, Ivan followed the wolf's tracks, which led, by an unfamiliar path, to the mouth of a vast and gloomy cavern. There he lost sight of them, and he was deliberating what to do next, when a loud peal of silvery laughter broke on his ears and awoke the silent echoes of the grim walls around him. Ivan started in open-mouthed astonishment. Standing before him was a girl more lovely—ten thousand times more lovely—than any woman he had hitherto seen. To the magic of a beautiful form in woman—the necromancy of female grace—there was no more ready and willing subject than Ivan; and here, at last, he had found grace personified, incarnate, the highest ideal of all his wildest and most cherished dreams. His most magnificent "castle" had never contained a princess half as fair as this one. Her figure was rather above the medium height, supple and slender. Her feet and hands were small, her wrists well rounded, her fingers long and white, and tipped with pink and glossy almond-shaped nails—if anything a trifle too long. But it was her face that so attracted Ivan as to almost hold him spellbound—the neat and delicately moulded features all in perfect harmony; the daintily cut lips; the white gleaming teeth; the low forehead crowned with golden curls; the long, thick-lashed, blue eyes that looked steadily into his, and seemed to read his very soul.

Moreover, in her blue eyes there was bewildering depth; a sense of coldness that was positively benumbing, and which was reminiscent of the blue petrifying waters of the Ural Lakes; a magnetism that was paralysing, that held in complete obeisance both mind and limb, and was comparable to nothing so nearly as the hypnotic influence of the tiger or snake, but which differed from the latter inasmuch as its inspirations were just as delightful as those of the tiger and snake are harrowing and terrifying.

She was clad from head to foot in fur—white fur—but neither her dress nor her presence excited any other thoughts in Ivan except those of intense admiration—admiration which surged through every pore of his skin.

"Well!" she demanded, "what brings you here, my good man? There is no game in this cave."

"Isn't there?" Ivan stammered, his eyes looking at her adoringly. "All the same I would cheerfully forgo all the pleasures of the chase to come here."

"You are very gallant for a huntsman, sir," the girl replied with a smile; "but for your own sake I must urge you to go away at once. I live here with my father—a confirmed recluse who detests the sight of human beings; were he to discover me talking to one I should get into sad trouble, and with regard to you I could not say what might happen."

But Ivan came of a race that paid little heed to any warning when once their blood was fired; consequently, despite the repeated admonitions of his beautiful companion—admonitions which her eyes seemed to contradict—he stayed and stayed, whilst—forgetful of mother and sisters, home, and even Dolk—he made a passionate avowal of his love. The afternoon quickly passed, and the sun was beginning to set, when the girl, whose name he had learned was Breda, almost pushed him out of the cavern.

"If you don't go now," she urged, "I may never see you again."

"And would you care?" he asked.

"Perhaps," she replied; "perhaps, just a little—a wee, wee bit. You see, I don't get the opportunity of meeting many people!"

He caught her by the hand and kissed it passionately; and with the sound of her light, intoxicating laughter thrilling through his soul, he descended to the bed of the mountain streamlet, and turned his steps blithely towards home.

That was the beginning, but not the end. He courted her—he married her and she came to live with his mother and sisters, who for his sake tried to like her and even pretended that they did like her. But in secret they said to one another, "She has no heart; she is cold as an icicle; her lips are thin and cruel. She would serve Ivan badly if we were not here to check her."

And Breda certainly had her idiosyncrasies. She preferred raw to cooked meat, and would not sleep in the same room as her husband. She grew very angry when Ivan expostulated, saying, "You promised you would never thwart me. If you do not keep your word, I shall despise you, scorn you, hate you." And Ivan, who loved his wife beyond anything, yielded.

Some weeks after their marriage, neighbours complained of losing cattle and horses. They said there was a wolf about, and that its tracks, which they had followed, always ended under the walls of Ivan's house. They asked Ivan if he had not heard the brute. But he had heard nothing, he slept very soundly. Then they inquired of Ivan's sisters and mother, who also replied in the negative; but there was hesitation in their voices, and they looked very frightened and ashamed. And then people began to talk. They looked at Breda curiously, and finally they cut her. One night, when there was a downfall of snow, and the wind howled down the chimneys of Ivan's house and blew the snow, with heavy thumps against the window-panes, Ivan, who could not sleep for the storm, heard the door of Breda's room open very softly, and light steps steal stealthily down the passage. Then there came a half-suppressed, half-smothered cry, a groan, and all was still. Ivan got out of bed and opened his door, but his wife's voice called to him from the darkness and bade him go back.

"Do not be alarmed and make a fuss," she said; "I was ill a moment ago, but am quite well again now. Go back to bed at once, or I shall be very angry." And Ivan obeyed her.

In the morning his eldest sister, Beata, was found dead in bed, her throat, breast, and stomach slit open, as is the custom with wolves, and her flesh all mangled and eaten.

Breda took no food that day, and Ivan's mother and other sister, Malvina, looked at her out of the corner of their eyes and shuddered. But Ivan said nothing. A week later the same fate befell Malvina. Then Ivan's mother spoke. She told him that he must assuredly be under some evil spell, or he would never remain idle whilst his sisters' destroyer was at large, and she adjured him, by all that he held holy, not to allow himself a moment's rest till he had had ample vengeance for the loss of two such valuable lives.

Roused at last, Ivan, instead of going to bed, sat up, gun in hand, and watched. He passed many nights thus, and his patience was well nigh exhausted when, during one of the vigils, he fell asleep, dreaming as usual of the blue eyes and golden curls of Breda, whose beauty held him just as much enthralled as ever. From this slumber he was awakened by loud screams for help. Seizing his gun, and taking a random aim at a huge white wolf as he went (though without stopping to see the effects of the shot), he ran to his mother's bedside. She was dead. Her throat and body were slit; but she was not eaten.

Wild with grief and thirsting for revenge, Ivan started off in pursuit of the wolf, and discovered, in the passage, a track of blood which terminated at his wife's door. Receiving no reply when he asked for admittance, he entered the room and found Breda lying on the floor, in her nightdress, the blood streaming from a wound in her shoulder. Ivan knelt down and examined her. She had been struck by a bullet, and the bullet fitted the bore of his gun.

He knew the truth then—the truth he might have known all along, had he not, in his blind love, thrust it far from him—and, in the sudden alteration of his feeling, he raised his knife to kill her. But Breda opened her eyes, and the weapon fell from his hand.

"You know part of my secret now," she whispered, "but you

don't know everything. I am a werwolf, not by inheritance, but of my own free will. In order to become one I ate the blue flowers in the wood. I did so to be avenged on my husband."

"Your husband!" Ivan cried; "good God! then you were a widow when I met you?"

"Yes," Breda said slowly and with apparent effort. "I was forced into my first marriage by my all too worldly parents, and my husband ill-used and beat me!"

"The devil! the cold-hearted, cowardly devil!" Ivan ejaculated, "I would have killed him."

"That is what I did," Breda remarked; "I did kill him, and it was in order to make certain of killing him that I became a werwolf."

"Did you eat him?" Ivan asked, horribly fascinated.

"Don't ask questions," Breda said, averting her eyes, "and for God's sake don't lose any more time. As you love me, screen me from detection; hide all traces of to-night's handiwork as quickly as possible."

As usual, Ivan did as she requested him, and giving out that his mother had died suddenly, from heart failure, he had her interred with as little publicity as possible.

Before very long, however, the neighbours began to ask such pointed questions, that Ivan now lived in a state of chronic suspense. He feared every moment that the truth would leak out, and that his beautiful young wife would receive condign punishment.

At last, finding such a state of apprehension intolerable, he confided in an old man who was reputed a sage and metaphysician—one who was extremely well versed in all matters appertaining to the spiritual world. “There is only one course to pursue,” the old man said, “you must have the evil spirit in her exorcized, and you must have it done immediately. Otherwise, she will continue her depredations, and your good neighbours will find her out and kill her. They more than half suspect her now, and are talking of paying a visit some night, when you are snug and safe in bed, to the cemetery, to see if the story you told them about your mother’s and sisters’ sudden deaths is correct.”

“What kind of exorcism would you use?” Ivan inquired nervously. “You would not hurt her?”

“The form of exorcism I should make use of would do her no lasting harm,” the old man said feelingly; “you can rely on me for that.”

“But is exorcism always effectual?” Ivan persisted.

“When exorcism is ineffectual it is the exception, not the rule,” the old man replied, “and there are very few cases of exorcism being employed ineffectually upon those who have become werwolves through the practice of magic, or the medium of flowers or of water.”

“Should my wife refuse to undergo the ceremony, what would you advise then?” Ivan asked.

“Strategy and force,” the old man said, “anything to prevent her continuing in her demoniacal ways, and being burned or drowned by an infuriated mob.”

Thus admonished, Ivan, without delay, broached the matter to Breda. But she was so angry with him for having dared even to mention exorcism, that he thought it best to act on the advice of the old occultist and to catch her unawares. Consequently, one evening, when the moon was in the full, and she had just changed into wolf form, he stole into her room accompanied by the old man and two assistants. After a desperate struggle, Ivan and the three exorcists overpowered her, and bound her so securely that she could not move.

They then took her out of doors, to a lonely spot at the back of the house, and placed her in the centre of an equilateral triangle that had been carefully marked on the ground, in red chalk. At seven or eight feet to the west of the triangle they then kindled a wood fire, and placed over it a vessel containing a fumigation mixture of hypericum, vinegar, sulphur, cayenne, and mountain ash berries.

The old man then knelt down, and crossing himself on his forehead and chest, prayed vigorously, until the preparation in the pot began to give off strong fumes. He then arose, and both he and his assistants took up specially prepared switches, cut from a mountain ash, and gripping them tightly in their hands, approached the recumbent form of the werwolf. This, however, was more than Ivan could stand—he had objected strongly enough to the fumigation, which, being nauseous and irritating, had made his wolf-wife gasp and choke; but when it came to flogging her—well, it turned him sick and cold. He forgot discretion, prudence, everything, saving the one great fact—monstrous, incredible, abominable—that the being he loved, adored, and worshipped was about to be beaten with rods! With a shout of wrath he rushed at the trio, and snatching their wands from them, laid them so soundly about their backs that they all three fled from the ground, shrieking with pain and terror. Then he knelt by his prostrate wife, and cutting the thongs that bound her, set her free. She rose on her feet a huge, white wolf. Regarding him steadily for a moment from out of her gleaming grey eyes, she swung slowly round, and with one more look, more human than animal, she darted swiftly away, and was speedily lost in the gloom.

The author

# Elliott O'Donnell

*"I have investigated, sometimes alone, and sometimes with other people and the press, many cases of reputed hauntings. I believe in ghosts, but am not a spiritualist."*

Elliott O'Donnell was a professional ghost hunter and prolific author, who produced an impressive series of books on ghosts and the paranormal. He claimed to have seen a ghost, described as an elemental figure covered with spots, when he was a five year old boy. Another claim of his was a strangulation attempt by a mysterious phantom, which attacked him in Dublin.

Elliott O'Donnell (27 February 1872 – 8 May 1965) was born in Clifton as the son of an Irish father, Rev. Henry O'Donnell (1827–1873) and an English mother Elizabeth Mousley. He had three older siblings, Henry, Helena and Petronella. After the birth of his fourth child the Rev. Henry O'Donnell travelled to Abyssinia while awaiting preferment to a new parish. Here he was alleged to have been attacked by a gang and robbed and slain.

O'Donnell was educated at Clifton College in Bristol, England, and later at Queen's Service Academy, Dublin, Ireland. After originally intending to take his entry exams at Sandhurst with a view to joining the

Royal Irish Constabulary (RIC), he travelled in the United States, working on a range in Oregon and becoming a policeman during the Chicago Railway Strike of 1894. After returning to England, he worked as a schoolmaster. In 1905 he married Ada O'Donnell (1870–1937).

His first book, written in his spare time, was a psychic thriller titled *For Satan's Sake* (1904). He composed several popular novels, including an occult fantasy, *The Sorcery Club* (1912), but specialized in true tales of ghosts and hauntings. At the time these were immensely popular. O'Donnell published in numerous magazines, including *Hutchinson Story Magazine, The Novel Magazine, The Idler, Weekly Tale-Teller, Hutchinson's Mystery-Story Magazine, Pearson's Magazine, Lilliput* and *Weird Tales.* As he became known as an authority on the supernatural, he was called upon more often as a ghost hunter. He also assisted in radio broadcasts on the paranormal in Britain and the United States.

Elliott O'Donnell died aged 93 at the Grosvenor Nursing Home at Clevedon in North Somerset on 8 May 1965.

■

## Bibliography


- *For Satan's Sake* (1904)
- *Unknown Depths* (1905)
- *Some Haunted Houses* (1908)
- *Haunted Houses of London* (1909)
- *Reminiscences of Mrs.E. M. Ward* (1910)
- *Byways of Ghostland* (1911)
- *The Meaning of Dreams* (1911)
- *Scottish Ghost Stories* (1912)
- *The Sorcery Club* (1912)
- *Werewolves* (1912)
- *Animal Ghosts* (1913)
- *Ghostly Phenomena* (1913)
- *Haunted Highways and Byways* (1914)
- *The Irish Abroad* (1915)
- *Twenty Years' Experience as a Ghost Hunter* (1916)
- *The Haunted Man* (1917)
- *Spiritualism Explained* (1917)
- *Fortunes* (1918)
- *Haunted Places in England* (1919)
- *Menace of Spiritualism* (1920)
- *More Haunted Houses of London* (1920)
- *Ghosts, Helpful and Harmful* (1924)
- *The Banshee* (1927)
- *Strange Disappearances* (1927)
- *Strange Sea Mysteries* (1927)
- *Confessions of a Ghost Hunter* (1928)
- *Great Thames Mysteries* (1929)
- *Famous Curses* (1929)
- *Fatal Kisses* (1929)
- *The Boys' Book of Sea Mysteries* (1930) Dodd, Mead & Company


'Elliott O'Donnell was a professional ghost hunter and prolific author.'

- *Rooms of Mystery* (1931) London: Philip Allan & Co. Ltd.
- *Ghosts of London* (1932)
- *The Devil in the Pulpit* (1932)
- *Family Ghosts* (1934)
- *Strange Cults & Secret Societies of Modern London* (1934)
- *Spookerisms; Twenty-five Weird Happenings* (1936)
- *Haunted Churches* (1939)
- *Ghosts with a Purpose* (1952)
- *Dead Riders* (1953)
- *Dangerous Ghosts* (1954)
- *Phantoms of the Night* (1956)

■

From the same author

***The Banshee***
*A Ghost Hunter's Investigation*
Elliot O'Donnell
222 pages, Paperback,
ISBN 9789492355232
www.vamzzz.com

The banshee is a mysterious female spirit in Irish folklore, who heralds the death of a family member, usually by shrieking or keening. The screeching sound is described as somewhere between the wail of a woman and the moan of an owl, a low singing or piercing loud and able to break glass.

The banshee appears as an old hag or beautiful lady, but may also appear in a variety of other forms, such as that of a crow, stoat, hare and weasel – animals associated in Ireland with witchcraft. The name *Banshee* seems to be a contraction of the Irish Bean Sidhe, which is interpreted by some writers on the subject as *A Woman of the Faire Race,* whilst by various other writers it is said to signify *The Lady of Death, The Woman of Sorrow, The Spirit of the Air,* or *The Woman of the Barrow.*

Elliott O'Donnell did a thorough investigation on the banshee – partly as a professional ghost hunter (with a personal encounter) – and wrote this fascinating special of paranormal literature.

VAMzzz Publishing

# Paper books

*VAMzzz Publishing* creates new and revised editions of books in the categories Magic & Witchcraft, Secret Rites & Societies, Demonology, Celtic & Mythology and Astrology. These books are written by either highly qualified academic researchers, or experts in a special field of esoteric knowledge, craft or practice.

As a publisher, we deeply respect the author of any book we choose and strive to work our own kind of magic in such a way, that it would put a smile on the author's faces, should they be watching us from heaven. In most of our books we offer 'Post Scriptum', aditional information about the author and/or the subject.

In contrast to the current trend of digital screen addiction, we think, this variety of literature needs to be presented on paper. *No e-books, but real books!*

Apart from republications of valuable but forgotten books, we also offer interesting articles on our occult blog: www.vamzzz.com/blog

Previews of all books, including a complete table of contents, can be viewed on www.vamzzz.com. More books will be added to the list in due time.

**VAMzzz Publishing**
P.O. Box 3340
1001 AC Amsterdam
The Netherlands
vamzzz@protonmail.com
www.vamzzz.com

***Vampires & Vampirism***
by Dudley Wright
160 pages, Paperback, ISBN 9789492355423

Wright explores the vampire phenomena in different parts of the world and in different times in our history, starting with ancient Babylonia, Assyria and Greece. He continues with the vampire in Great Britain and the British Empire, Germany and it's surrounding countries, Bavaria, Hungary, Silesia, Bulgaria and Russia. The vampire in literature is also treated and the volume ends with the fact or fiction question.

***Thirty Years Among the Dead***
by Dr. Carl A. Wickland
554 pages, Paperback, ISBN 9789492355447

Wickland's dedicated research, in combination with the excellent medium-ship of Anna, has resulted in one the most fascinating and taboo-breaking works on spiritualism and life after death-questions ever. Perhaps today the book is even more actual than it was in it's publication year 1924. The mystery of death touches all of us, while the general climate for the development of spiritual intelligence is worsening to levels that should concern all of us deeply.

***Human Leopards***
*An Account of the Trials of Human Leopards Before the Special Commission*
by K.J. Beatty
210 pages, paperback ISBN 9789492355492

The early 20th century showed an increase number of occult murders by the Human Leopard Society of Sierra Leone. The main reason for the killings was to obtain human fat for anointing a terrible fetish called the Borfima, whose black magic depended on the frequency with which it was "fed." These killings got mixed with ritual cannibalism, of which the first reports for this area date back to 1609.

www.ingramcontent.com/pod-product-compliance
Ingram Content Group UK Ltd.
Pitfield, Milton Keynes, MK11 3LW, UK
UKHW042007190726
13854UKWH00005B/2204

9 789492 355508